MW01231978

Income Allocation

Enhance Your Retirement Security

David L. Gaylor

Copyright ©2017, David Gaylor.

ISBN: 978-0-9990189-0-3

All Rights Reserved. No part of this book may be reproduced or transmitted in any form or by any means, electronic or mechanical, including photocopying, recording, or by any information storage and retrieval system without written permission from the author, except for the inclusion of brief quotations in a review.

Printed in the United States of America.

ACKNOWLEDGMENTS

Becoming an author was never one of my life's ambitions. However, not long ago as I was enjoying a good book, the thought crossed my mind, "I wonder what it is like to write a book?" The process was intriguing to me, and I became very curious about how an author goes about their work. Personally, it all started with a simple observation regarding two different prospective clients a few years back. This observation grew first into an idea, and then a theory, and finally after much research and study, it became a tangible plan that I've been able to implement for many clients. It is this concept that I share here with you, in the pages that follow.

It's been a very interesting and engaging process. There were also many sizable and unforeseen challenges along the way as well as a commitment of both time and resources that I could not possibly have been prepared for. For these reasons and many more, I would like to express my sincere gratitude to several key people, without whom this work would not be possible.

First, to my wife, my high school sweetheart and soulmate Mitzi, who offers endless encouragement and strength, many times without even knowing you're doing it. You blessed me by agreeing to spend your life with me. Almost 30 years later and with three grown children, one granddaughter and two more grandchildren on the way, I couldn't imagine what my life would be like if you had said no instead of yes so many years ago. Thank you my love, for understanding me and encouraging me, but most of all, tolerating me!

My children, Aubrey, Abby and Brady—the young adults you've turned into amazes me every day. You're the inspiration that motivates me on a daily basis, and I'm so thankful that God allowed me to be your Dad. The world is be a better place because of each one of you, and I can't wait to see what you will accomplish. Don't settle for ordinary because each one of you is exceptional!

My business partners and two of my best friends in the world, Gary Reed and Rodney Harris. Thank you for your confidence in and support of this project and for allowing both time and resources to be allocated to it. Since we met in 2002, you both have become like brothers to me, and not a day goes by that I don't give thanks that we met, became friends, and then business partners. You guys are truly the best. My family and I have been greatly blessed since the day the two of you came into our lives.

My two lieutenants in Atlanta, Chad Gough and Kevin Hale, for their invaluable assistance in helping me to re-engineer how I express certain ideas and concepts, in the interest of having a more compliance-friendly final product. Without your help this project might have lost momentum and fallen by the wayside because in all honesty, these were some of the most trying times that I would encounter on this journey. Thank you both for taking charge and for helping me to realize a more polished final product.

A big thank you, Maggie Haverty. Maggie always keeps me on point and coordinates all of my various projects. How you keep it all straight Maggie, I will never know.

My great friends Chris McIntire, Don Cloud, Tom O'Connell, Ralph Grauso and Scott Moore. Having you all there to bounce ideas off of was instrumental, as was your willingness to listen as I worked my way through some of the challenges I faced. Your friendship means the world to me, guys. Each of you played a big part in this book becoming a reality. Thank you.

Thank you to all of the financial professionals at 3-Mentors, Inc. We are all very much a family and I appreciate every one of you for allowing me to be a part of each of your lives, and to be your Mentor. Your various successes inspire me on a daily basis to continue to develop new processes and tools that assist you to help your clients achieve their financial and retirement visions.

Finally, to all my clients in the Sidney, Ohio, area. Thank you for the trust you've shown me over the years. It is a responsibility that I do not take lightly and one of the primary reasons that I wrote this book. Witnessing your individual retirement journeys over the years, the challenges you've faced and shared with me, the joys you've realized and also shared with me, have made my career thus far an incredibly rewarding experience. It's what makes each day that I go to work so exciting. It truly is a privilege to serve you.

FOREWORD

When I first met David in 2015, I was both inspired and impressed, and felt an immediate connection with "The Professor," as he is known in financial circles. He is gifted at making complex topics easier to understand, putting into words concepts that had previously been challenging to explain. Combine that with his passion to share his knowledge with anyone willing to listen, and "The Professor" moniker makes perfect sense.

My wife, Paula, and I love boating, and we spend much of our free time on the St. Croix River. It's a big river, but navigation is pretty straightforward. Head a couple hours southeast, however, and you'll hit the Mighty Mississippi. The Mississippi River lives up to its name, there are locks and dams, wing dams and river markers that must be adhered to. So good navigation tools are crucial.

Like the Mississippi, the waters of the financial world can be a little confusing if you don't know where you're going. This book helps you navigate those waters. In it, The Professor clearly leads you through the need for guaranteed income in retirement. It's vital for people to understand that their retirement may last 30-40 years, and I believe that society has done an inadequate job of educating the average American citizen. In over 30 years in the financial services industry, I have found that most retirees I work with are not just concerned about running out of money; they're fearful of running out of income, which is why I have always believed in income as a first priority in retirement. And, why I believe in this book you're holding now.

When I sit down with someone and introduce the concept of helping solve their retirement income needs with just a portion of their portfolio, leaving the balance available for an investment strategy, I can see the sense of relief in their eyes when they get it. That's one of the most satisfying aspects of what I do: seeing that "ah ha" moment when clients relax, knowing that their income will be there throughout their entire retirement. It can be an emotional moment. That's why I believe that Income Allocation is what retirement is all about – David has basically laid out a map of how to do retirement right and not make it so complicated.

The only decision that you can make better than the one you've already made in picking up this book is to read it cover-to-cover. The most generous decision you can make is to share this with your family and friends when you are finished reading it.

I wish all of you a successful, comfortable and happy retirement.

- Donald L. Reynolds
President, Strategic Asset Preservation, Inc.

TABLE OF CONTENTS

INTRODUCTION

SURVIVING YOUR RESOURCES

On the day I sit down to write the beginning pages of this book, statistically[1] 10,000 Baby Boomers are turning age 66: full retirement age now for Social Security benefits. On the day you read the opening pages of this book, another 10,000 or so are turning retirement age. It really doesn't matter when you're reading these pages as long as it's before the year 2031, because that's the year the last of the Baby Boomers, those born in 1964, will reach full retirement age (then 67) and will be able to claim their full Social Security benefits. I'm one of those people—I was born in 1964—so what I'm writing about in this book is of extreme importance to me, my friends and my family members.

MORE SECURITY FOR THE AMERICAN FAMILY
THE SOCIAL SECURITY ACT AS AMENDED OFFERS GREATER OLD-AGE INSURANCE PROTECTION TO PEOPLE NOW NEARING RETIREMENT AGE
SOCIAL SECURITY BOARD

As thousands of Boomers become retirees, a question comes to mind. No, not the politically charged, "How will the federal government and the Social Security Administration (SSA) address the long-term solvency issues of Social Security," when according to the 2015 Social Security Board of Trustees' Report:[2]

[1] United States of America. Census Bureau, Department of Commerce. By Sandra Colby and Jennifer Ortman. The Baby Boom Cohort in the United States: 2012 to 2060. U.S. Census Bureau, May 2014. Web. 19 Dec. 2014.

[2] United States of America. The Social Security Administration. The 2015 Annual Report of the Board of Trustees of the Federal Old—Age and Survivors Insurance and Federal Disability Insurance Trust Funds. The 2015 OASDI Trustees Report. The Social Security Administration, 22 July 2015. Web. 3 Feb. 2015. https://www.ssa.gov/oact/TR/2015/tr2015.pdf

"Under current law, the projected cost of Social Security increases faster than projected income through 2037 primarily because of the aging of the baby boom generation and relatively low fertility since the baby-boom period. Cost will continue to grow faster than income after 2037, but to a lesser degree, due to increasing life expectancy. Based on the Trustees' intermediate assumptions, program cost exceeds non-interest income for 2015, as it has since 2010, and remains higher than non-interest income throughout the remainder of the 75-year projection period."

The answer to that question would require another book and a different author. However, it is a genuine social issue and one that must be addressed. It is certain to be among the top debated issues during the next several elections.

No, the question on my mind this Saturday night is this: "How many of those people are facing the likelihood of living beyond the exhaustion of their retirement resources?"

Have you ever heard anyone say, "I anticipate a retirement that endures long after the resources I've worked my entire adult life to accumulate have been exhausted?" Not one person has ever said that to me, and I suspect that no one reading this book has ever heard anything like this either. I have heard many goals for retirement over the years as an investment advisor: traveling the world, reinvention of self, starting an entirely different career, spending time as a volunteer for the causes that are close to my heart, playing golf seven days a week, enjoying a second home in a different place, going back to college and learning something new, spending the winters somewhere warm, spending the summers somewhere cool, you name it, I've heard it. Yet no one has ever indicated to me that they are anticipating depletion of savings before the end of their days. If that's not the case, then why are so many facing this same scenario during retirement?

As a United States citizen, a financial advisor, a fiduciary, and as a human being, I am highly concerned about the possibility that millions of people retiring over the next 20 to 30 years will face making lifestyle adjustments, versus enjoying their long-planned and diligently worked-for retirement.

WHY THE WELLS RUN DRY

When I ask myself why it is that many retirees are facing the possibility of outliving their resources, many answers came to mind. Thanks to advances in medicine, people today are living longer, much longer in fact than their parents and grandparents.[3] Lifetime pensions have seen a steep decline within the last 20 to 30 years, and their numbers dwindle each year.[4] Yields on traditional savings vehicles are negligible in the low interest rate environment we have been in for some time now. Already in this century, we have endured two substantial bear markets that have devastated many portfolios and even compelled some to exit the market entirely or in part, essentially forgoing participation in the subsequent recoveries. Those answers are all true, and you probably can think of many more.

To me, though, one of the biggest factors (if not THE biggest) contributing to the portfolio depletion issue, is that so many people have been given erroneous guidance. Retirement income planning guidance has been given with

[3] "Are You Ready? What You Need to Know about Ageing." World Health Organization. The United Nations, n.d. Web. 19 Dec. 2014. http://www.who.int/world-health-day/2012/toolkit/background/en/

[4] The United States. The Social Security Administration. The Office of Retirement and Disability Policy & The Office of Research, Evaluation, and Statistics. The Disappearing Defined Benefit Pension and Its Potential Impact on the Retirement Incomes of Baby Boomers. By Howard M. Iams, Barbara A. Butrica, Karen E. Smith, and Eric J. Toder. 3rd ed. Vol. 69. Washington: Social Security Administration, 2009. Print. 13-11700.

good intentions, but—unbeknownst to the one providing the direction—was based on retirement planning theory that would later be shown to have an inherent flaw, specifically for those with the misfortune of starting retirement during certain periods in the economic cycle. The flaw I speak of is that these retirement planning doctrines fail to account for the very real hazard known as "Sequence Risk."[5]

> Sequence Risk is defined as:
> *The risk of receiving lower or negative returns early in a period when withdrawals are made from the underlying investments. The order—or sequence—of investment returns is a primary concern for those individuals who are retired and living off the income and capital of their investments.*

It's all about timing. Asset Allocation and the 4% Rule, the prevalent retirement income planning methodologies of recent history, do not account for one very important variable, *the order (or timing)* of returns. These models are based solely on long-term *average returns*. We now know that failing to account for this variable can carry significant consequences, particularly for those who experience severe, multiple, and/or prolonged recessionary market cycles in the earlier years of their retirement. William Bengen, the financial planner who developed *the 4% Rule*[6] in 1994, has refuted the practicality of his own theory. In a May 2012 article in Financial Advisor magazine,[7] Bengen states, "Research has confirmed that the 'sequence of investment returns' is crucial for portfolio longevity; a retiree with low returns early in retirement will probably have trouble later in retirement."

Some would say that Mr. Bengen's partial repudiation still downplays (or at least underestimates) the potential for some considerable shortfalls.

---

5 "Sequence Risk Definition | Investopedia." Investopedia. Investopedia, LLC, 13 May 2008. Web. 15 Dec. 2014.

6 Bengen, William P. "Determining Withdrawal Rates Using Historical Data." Journal of Financial Planning (1994): 171-80. Print.

7 Bengen, William P. "How Much Is Enough?" Financial Advisor 1 May 2012. Financial Advisor. Web. 18 Dec. 2014. http://www.fa-mag.com/news/how-much-is-enough-10496.html

Regardless, think about that for a moment. Two identically constructed portfolios, designed for the same purpose of generating retirement income and experiencing both the same exact yearly and average returns, might have life cycles that differ significantly, depending on the timing and severity of losses that are realized early in retirement. Potentially, one portfolio falls several years short of reaching its primary goal of generating income for a 30 year retirement, while the other not only accomplishes this goal, but actually leaves an *appreciated* value for beneficiaries.

In other words, Asset Allocation and The 4% Rule may well have worked as prescribed for many—those fortunate enough to retire and then experience economic growth in the early years—but as I said before, it's all about timing. Personally, I am constitutionally incapable of leaving that much to chance, not for myself, not for my family, and certainly not for those who have entrusted me as their fiduciary, with the honor of guiding them as they prepare financially for the final stage of their journey.

SET FOR LIFE

The good news, though, is that retirement at or below the poverty level is not a forgone conclusion. Many retirees live comfortably for decades after their paychecks stop, and rarely is it because they've managed to accumulate or inherit a small fortune, or had the vision to buy Apple's common stock at less than a buck-fifty back in 1982.

Let me introduce you to a married couple who are clients of mine. Let's call them "Adam and Beth Walker."[8] They are 61 and 59 years old, respectively. 'Adam' is planning to retire in five years, while 'Beth' is slightly more than six years from her planned workforce exit.

[8] Fictitious names have been used for privacy purposes. The experiences of these individuals is not intended to be representative of what your experience might be and is no guarantee of future success.

The Walkers calculate that in addition to their Social Security benefits, they will need approximately $40,000 per year in order to support the retirement that they have planned. Their accumulated retirement savings total $1 million. I introduced the Walkers to a strategy that I've implemented for many of my clients, one that utilizes fixed index annuities (FIAs) from some very well-known, established, and financially sound U.S. insurance companies.

The consideration that the Walkers will receive for placing only half of those liquid assets, or $500,000, is a guarantee backed by the financial strength and claims paying ability of the insurance company issuing the contract. Under this guarantee, not only is their principal and credited interest protected, but once they retire they will receive approximately $40,000 per year, as long as either is alive.

Fixed index annuities are designed for this very purpose. They are intended to meet long-term needs for retirement income and they also provide guarantees against loss of principal and credited interest. They also offer the reassurance of a death benefit for the beneficiaries of the owner(s).

So now the Walkers have established an income stream for life equal to their projected needs, and they did so by utilizing only half of their retirement savings. The other half, $500,000, can now be used for any purpose they want: travel, discretionary purchases, a vacation home, investing in potentially high-return ventures.

Indeed, with savvy investing that $500,000 could become $1 million again someday. Meanwhile, the Walkers will still have the annual income stream needed to cover their living expenses from the first part of their savings, each and every year of retirement.

The primary concession that the Walkers agree to comes in the form of a commitment to what is known as a "surrender schedule." This concession means that in the earliest years of the contract (typically the first 5 to 10 years), should any of the committed funds be accessed prior to the end of that surrender schedule, the amount withdrawn in excess of the yearly allowable, or "free withdrawal," amount (currently averaging 10%), would incur a surrender fee that is calculated as a percentage of (and only on) the excess amount.

A current seven year surrender schedule on a typical product today might look a lot like this:

Year One:	8%
Year Two:	7%
Year Three:	6%
Year Four:	5%
Year Five:	4%
Year Six:	3%
Year Seven:	2%

Now, let's take a wild turn and, for the sake of this demonstration, flash forward in time three-and-a-half years. We will pretend that the Walkers somehow managed to part ways with their first $500,000 already. Remember, $500,000 of the $1 million that they had accumulated for retirement was essentially made accessible to them to use as they wish, just by way of employing this strategy in the first place. It is now three-and-a-half years since the Walkers agreed to and executed this plan and now they need to access, say, $60,000.

This particular contract, and many like it today, carries a 10% per year (after the first year) free-withdrawal allowance. Thus, after the first year, $50,000 is off the table, leaving $10,000 of the $60,000 withdrawal in our example to be assessed for the early surrender charge. The schedule calls for a 6% charge in the third year, so this unplanned emergency need to access $60,000 in cash would only cost $600 ($10,000 x .06= $600) in surrender charges. In my opinion, I don't think there would be lower transaction costs involved in another alternative format, venue, or vehicle established or utilized for the same purpose, had the Walkers gone a different route in their retirement planning. Please be aware, if the clients in this example were to take a free withdrawal prior to triggering the $40,000 guaranteed lifetime joint income payment that we outlined earlier, this could potentially reduce the amount of their guaranteed joint income payout in the future depending on specific product features and benefits.

In Chapter Two, I'll go into more detail about this plan that I employed with the Walkers, which I call "Income Allocation." For now, keep in mind that it is possible to get the reliable, steady income you require to meet your needs over an extended retirement without having to employ 100% of your life savings in order to generate this income. It is my hope that you will see the wisdom in a plan such as this.

I'm going to show you that people of average (even above average) means who intend to fund an entire 30 year retirement's income needs by using the more customary methods will generally need to utilize their entire retirement savings in order to have a more favorable chance of doing so. Either that, or they will need to realize some amazing investment returns in the future.

Want to make a major purchase? If you do, you'll be depleting your income base! Spend too much early on in retirement, or suffer a multi-year market correction while doing so, and you could face a significant increase in the risk of outliving your resources.

ADVISOR AGENDAS

The question I have for you and for everyone else

currently in, or planning for, retirement is this: with such a strategy available—one that can provide a predictable stream of retirement income and doesn't require 100% of your life savings—why aren't more people directed to this strategy? This strategy that could potentially free up part of your savings for those special things—the trip of a lifetime, that beach condo or motor home or dream car—without depleting your income base. I'll explain this strategy to you in the pages of this book.

In my opinion, the answer to why many people aren't advised of this strategy is apparent: the advisors and brokers with whom they are working are still practicing the aforementioned doctrines, even though these doctrines are now widely considered to be inherently flawed. Those advisors may try to discredit this book and the underlying theory but ask yourself, "Why they would do that?" Why would they cling to a model that has the potential to elevate one's risk of outliving their retirement resources?

Most likely, the answer lies in where they work. The unfortunate reality is that many if not most financial services firms dictate the products that their advisors can access and thus are able to offer to their clients, because of their contractual relationships.

This creates a dilemma, whereby advisors with the intention to honor their fiduciary responsibility to act in the best interest of their clients simply do not have access to certain products. That's because their firm does not have the requisite selling agreement(s) in place with the product sponsor, even though the advisors may consider a particular product to be better suited to meet the objectives of certain clients, more so than what they currently can access within the firm where they are registered.

Here's a quick preview into the power of my favored strategy, which will be thoroughly explained later on.

If I invest $500,000 in a "typical" portfolio, in 10 years how much income can I take from it without violating basic financial planning fundamentals and therefore increasing my risk of eventually depleting my resources? The answer is, I have no idea!

Past performance isn't going to guarantee some future value. I work with some outstanding private wealth managers who invest my clients' growth money, so I'm not against using financial markets, and I do not have a bias in favor of a particular product. In fact, I love the financial markets and the way my own money and my clients' money is managed!

Nevertheless, I am uncertain about how the markets will perform over the next 10 years. If clients double their money, that $500,000 will become $1,000,000. Current fundamentals show that if a client retires at age 66, he or she can prudently withdraw about $30,000 in the first year. With the strategy I'm going to explain to you, some of today's favored products in particular would allow a married couple to utilize $500,000 at age 56 to create an income stream of over $38,000, starting at age 66 and contractually guaranteed for life by the insurance company. That's assuming that over the intervening 10 years the money in this product doesn't earn one bit of growth.

COMPARATIVE ADVANTAGE

Think about that for a moment: 100% growth over an entire decade in the average portfolio constructed using the standard asset allocation model, from $500,000 to $1 million, would provide less income, fundamentally speaking, than one vehicle could—*and* this vehicle carries contractual guarantees. Once again, the preceding assumes a growth rate of zero but has the potential to be a number north of there (but *never* negative).

With that in mind, where do you think you might have the greater likelihood of securing your retirement income needs? The average portfolio constructed via the traditional asset allocation model and mobilized for income by way of employing the 4% Rule, would need to appreciate to $950,000, which equates to 90% growth in just ten years in order to generate the same income stream that one of the products described above could provide when an income rider is added.[9]

There are some products available as of the writing of this book that offer contractual guarantees plus an opportunity for growth that correlates to (but does not participate directly in) appreciation in the values of the investment market indexes selected.[10]

In those products, even if we assume a modest indexed interest rate of 3%, this married couple would receive $50,000 in the first year of their retirement. Under the 4% Rule, they'd need a portfolio valued at over $1,250,000 to provide that same level of cash flow, and under a more conservative 3% application, the portfolio would need to hold assets valued at nearly $1,700,000.

So I pose the question once more: "Where do you think you might have the greater likelihood to secure the income you'll need in retirement?"

Keep in mind, products change over time, and the versions described here may be quite different by the time you are reading this book. The basics however are likely to remain the same, which is why I intend to present to you an alternative approach to retirement income planning which I truly believe to have real potential to enhance both your retirement and general well-being.

---

[9] Income benefit riders are generally optional and available at an additional cost.

[10] With the purchase of an additional-cost riders, the contract's value will be reduced by the cost of the rider. This may result in a loss of principal and interest in any year in which the contract does not earn interest or earns interest in an amount less than the rider charge. This illustration does not take into account surrender charges which may apply to early withdrawals.

CHAPTER ONE

GRASPING THE GENERATION GAP

If you're a relatively young retiree or a pre-retiree, you might wonder what all the fuss is about. After all, your parents may have lived very comfortably in retirement (and might still be doing so), with nary a concern about running out of money. That's true, but things have changed. The circumstances your parents faced are very different than those facing today's retirees.

ROUGH BEGINNINGS, HAPPIER ENDINGS

If you're in the Baby Boomer generation (born in the late 1940s through the early 1960s), your parents probably were born in the first four decades of the 20th century. People born then are typically thought to belong to the "Greatest Generation" (grew up during World War I and fought or provided homeland support during World War II) or the "Silent Generation" (grew up during the Great Depression and World War II).

Many members of those generations went to work after finishing school, then spent most or all of their working careers with one employer. As a result, they often received pensions at retirement. In technical lingo, those pensions were and still are the fruits of defined benefit plans. In these plans, pensions are funded by employer contributions. The payouts last for a lifetime, no matter how long that might be, and there's usually a pension for a surviving spouse.

For people born from 1900 to 1940, the husband generally was the family breadwinner while the wife was the homemaker. If the husband earned a pension and died first, which typically was the case, the widow often continued to collect a survivor's lifetime benefit.

Don't forget, retirees started to receive Social Security payments in 1940. Thus, many members of preceding generations received lifelong benefits from the federal government as well as from a former employer. Together, Social Security and a pension might have equaled most or even all of the amount a retired couple earned during their years of employment. No wonder many people from that generation didn't (and still don't) worry about running out of money.

LOW SPENDING, HIGH YIELDS

Other factors contributed to the relative comfort previous generations have enjoyed in retirement. Having lived through the Great Depression, many members of those generations developed frugal spending habits.

What's more, there weren't as many things to spend money on. When people retired in, say, the 1960s or 1970s, they weren't concerned about how to keep up with the latest smartphone plans. Obviously, there were exceptions. However, many members of the Greatest Generation and the Silent Generation spent carefully during their working years and saved significant amounts.

Often, savings went into bank accounts and U.S. Savings Bonds, where yields usually were decent and sometimes extraordinary. Any stock market investments probably were helped by the bull market that lasted, with few setbacks, from 1982 until 2000, and saw the Dow Jones Industrial Average increase by over 1,400%, from 777 to 11,723! Obviously, even if you had to spend from your portfolio during this time period it wasn't much of a challenge. It was during this remarkable period of investment growth that the 4% Rule was established.

AGE-OLD ASSURANCE

As an example of the Greatest Generation, consider Charlie Thomson,[11] now age 94. Charlie served in World War II and had a successful career as an executive with a moderate income. Charlie retired at age 62, just in time to for his retirement portfolio to benefit from the bull markets of the 1980s and 1990s.

Charlie and his wife Debbie[11] have lived comfortably for decades on their Social Security checks and Charlie's pension. (As an additional benefit, Charlie's former employer also provides retiree health coverage, which combines with Medicare to cover medical bills.)

Charlie has some money in an IRA, and he reluctantly has taken the required minimum distribution (RMD) each year, paying the resulting income tax. Besides these RMDs, Charlie and Debbie have never needed to withdraw a penny from their savings for basic lifestyle needs. When I asked Charlie how they managed to live for 32 years on his pension and their Social Security checks alone, he told me that they actually save money from those income sources!

Charlie still plays golf, mows his lawn, and enjoys freedom from financial fears. He has his pension and his Social Security, and that income will be more than adequate for him. Knowing that their bills will be covered by those guaranteed income sources; Charlie and Debbie

[11] These characters are fictional and their reference is for illustrative purposes only. Your actual experience will vary.

have gone and are still going through their extended retirement with no concerns over their finances.

Think about that for a moment: retired for 32 years, waking up every day of every month knowing the bills are sure to be paid! This is an example of why I think the Greatest Generation has been, and continues to be, the most financially secure generation I will ever see. Indeed, one of my personal financial goals is to have the same comfort level for my wife and myself. Similarly, that's the goal I have for as many of my clients as possible and is the sole purpose of this book.

If you think Charlie's story is unusual, consider a representative of the Silent Generation: Ed Samuels,[12] now age 76. Ed worked in a machine shop in a small town and took early retirement at age 56.

Ed also receives a pension that has served him well for 20 years, in addition to the Social Security benefits he now receives. These cash flows have allowed Ed and his wife Florence[12] to live the same lifestyle they enjoyed prior to retiring, without ever having to tap into their savings.

Now that he is past the age 70½ mark, Ed must take required minimum distributions (RMDs) from his IRA. Ed doesn't like doing so—he loathes the idea of paying more tax than necessary—so he withdraws no more than the amount he is required to take out, in order to avoid a 50% penalty by the IRS.

For retirees like Charlie and Ed, Social Security benefits plus pension income have provided more than enough cash flow to cover their living expenses. Indeed, for all retirees—present and future—having adequate assured income provides a certain degree of security.

Once income has been secured, the remainder of savings becomes a luxury: you can spend these funds or pass them on. However, as we'll see in future chapters, many Baby Boomers lack the guaranteed income that their

[12] These characters are fictional and their reference is for illustrative purposes only. Your actual experience will vary.

parents enjoyed in the form of pensions, so they may not have similar stories of retirement income security to relate.

PRESENT IMPERFECT

Compared to prior generations, today's younger retirees and pre-retirees are less likely to have worked for decades with the same employer. Moreover, very few companies today provide the same defined benefit plan that Charlie and Ed had. Today companies have "defined contribution" plans like a 401(k).

With these plans, the payout in retirement is determined by the amount contributed to the plan as well as the investment performance after the contribution. The 2000-2002 and the 2008-2009 bear markets have reduced the amounts in such accounts considerably.

Therefore, today's defined contribution plans have uncertain payouts—the amounts can be disappointing. By comparison, yesterday's defined benefit plans that covered Charlie and Ed were designed to pay retired workers a given amount, no matter how markets performed.

Moreover, defined contribution plans are largely funded by employees themselves. Employers may make matching contributions, but such contributions are modest or, in many cases, nonexistent. Savings yields are low now and may stay there for the foreseeable future. With unpredictable retirement plans and scant savings yields, Baby Boomers who maintain a familiar lifestyle in retirement might well run short of money if they live into their 80s, 90s or beyond.

This book is intended to present an alternative strategy, using a different approach to solving the retirement challenge, rather than rely upon flawed theories that have been taken as fact by so many during the last 20 years.

Please spend some time with me inside the pages of this book and see if a different path is appropriate for you, a friend, or a family member. This path, or strategy, is intended to provide those who follow it with a more financially certain retirement. One where their income needs are anticipated and met each month by using only a portion of lifelong savings.

The portion necessary to meet those income needs could be as much as 70% or even 80% of investable assets. Even if it is that much—and it usually isn't—once retirees' income needs are met they can spend freely from the remainder of their assets or continue to invest the balance. With enough time and sufficient growth, retirees can generate the income they need in retirement from a reliable source and potentially replenish their portfolios to their former levels.

CHAPTER TWO

INCOME ALLOCATION FOR A RELAXED RETIREMENT

The concept of Income Allocation grew out of my learning about Sequence Risk, also known as Order of Return Risk, or Sequence of Return Risk. To keep things simple, I'll just refer to this concept as *sequence risk.*

In short, sequence risk means that the chronological order of investment returns is a crucial consideration, especially so for the newly retired who are drawing income from their portfolios. For non-retirees, the importance of sequence risk is modest—mainly a matter of opportunity cost—but for newer retirees, sequence risk has the potential to have a considerably negative impact on the lifespan of their retirement portfolios.

RUNNING THE NUMBERS

Let's set the stage. If you work with a financial advisor, or if you read investment publications, you may have heard or read a statement such as, "Historically, the market has generated an average annualized return of 8% over the last 20 years, or 9% over the last century."

The actual numbers may vary slightly, but they're basically true. Morningstar's subsidiary Ibbotson is widely considered to be one of the leading sources for historical investment return data and index averages.

According to Ibbotson,[13] "large company stocks" (which make up most of the value of the U.S. stock market) had compound annual returns of 9.9% for the 20 years from 1995 through 2014. Going all the way back to the beginning of the Ibbotson data base in 1926, large company stocks have returned 10.1% per year.

Those numbers are purely hypothetical, as they assume constant dividend reinvestment, no taxes, and no transaction costs. Nevertheless they do indicate that over time, a patient investor can earn an average annual return in the neighborhood of 8% to 9% which according to the Rule of 72,[14] means you can double your money in approximately eight to nine years.

EXCESSIVE EXPECTATIONS

Reliance on such statistics can lead to precarious expectations. Many investors consequently anticipate a steady 8% or 9% annual return. However, such steady and dependable market returns are not going to happen in the real world.

Instead, returns will vary significantly year over year. The broad market, as represented by the benchmark S&P 500® Index, might have a series of calendar year returns such as +27%, +9%, +6% and -15%.

With those returns, someone who invested $100,000 at the beginning of Year One would end the four years with $124,725.43: a compound annualized return of around 5.6%. Again, we'll disregard taxes, fees, and transaction costs to keep things simple.

Now let's reverse those calendar year returns and say the -15% happens in the first year, followed by +6%, +9%, and +27% annual returns. That sequence also produces the same 5.6% annualized return and the same

[13] Ibbotson Associates. Ibbotson SBBI 2013 Classic Yearbook: Market Results for Stocks, Bonds, Bills, and Inflation 1926-2012. Classic ed. Chicago, IL: Morningstar, 2013. Print.

[14] The Rule of 72 tells us that dividing the number 72 by a given rate of interest will provide the approximate number of years necessary to double the principal amount. This reference is given to demonstrate mathematical principles only and should not be regarded as absolute. Furthermore, the periodic declines in markets will result in diminishing the effective application of the Rule of 72.

amount of money: a $100,000 investment will grow to $124,725.43.

Indeed, it doesn't matter how many years' returns you use or how wide the variations may be. As long as you're in the accumulation phase and you stay invested, you'll get an annualized return that reflects the value of the gains and losses, but not the sequence in which they occurred.

WITHDRAWAL PAINS

Now let's shift the focus from the accumulation phase to the income phase of retirement, which is when you begin taking withdrawals for retirement spending needs. *That little fact is a game changer.*

For example, assume the same annual rates of return from the previous example (+27%, +9%, +6% and -15%) are experienced by two retirees, in a continuing loop. One retiree experiences the returns in the above order, but the other retiree starts with the negative year, followed by increasingly larger positive returns.

Both retirees start with exactly the same amount of money and withdraw exactly the same amount each year; both earn the same annualized rates of return over each four-year period.

However, one of the two investors runs out of money 13 years before the other! As you might expect, the one with the first-year negative return suffered the accelerated depletion of retirement funds.

That is Sequence Risk.

The message is that when you begin taking withdrawals from your savings for cash flow in retirement, loss management becomes critical. The significance of the ten years surrounding the date of your retirement is tremendous and cannot be emphasized enough. I've often heard this period of time referred to as the retirement "red zone."

What a great phrase—I think it sums up those crucial 10 years perfectly!

In my opinion, it is the misuse of long-term average return numbers that makes those 10 years so precarious. Many advisors and mutual fund companies point to long-term returns and urge investors to buy and hold.

They advise investors to stay the course in the midst of some painful bear markets with statements such as, "It's only a paper loss, hang in there, the market will come back, just as it has each time before."

Now, it's true that most major market indexes have recovered from setbacks. However, large losses of principal *while withdrawing from a portfolio* can prove disastrous to a retiree's financial security. This is a matter of mathematics and not an opinion or bias. Don't let anyone tell you differently.

DOUBLE TROUBLE

As I said before, Americans are living longer today and life expectancy is still on the rise. Many retirees today will live into their late 80s, 90s, and even reach triple digits. An extended retirement, of course, will contribute to the risk of running short of money at some point.

Therefore, sequence risk and longevity risk are two of the more significant risks to retirement income security that a retiree might encounter. What's more, they feed into each other.

Suppose Jane Parker[15] retires at 65 and begins drawing income from her portfolio. In an unfortunate turn of events, a prolonged bear market begins just she retires.

[15] This character is fictional and her reference is for illustrative purposes only. Your actual experience will vary.

If she dies in under 10 years, the longevity of her portfolio will be a moot point.

On the other hand, Jane could live to 80, 90, or even longer. After experiencing the bear market early into retirement, each dollar she withdraws from her savings for income will increase her risk of a premature depletion of her portfolio.

I believe (a) that retirees should be confident of meeting their income needs from a predictable source, regardless of market performance, and (b) that a vital stream of cash should keep flowing as long as the individual, or couple, lives.

I designed Income Allocation as a concept to better define these retirement income security ideals and to provide a proven strategy for overcoming longevity risk and sequence risk as potential roadblocks to that end.

UPS AND DOWNS

Planning for a reliable, lifelong retirement income stream may not sound like the most exciting of concepts to some individuals, such as those who are fond of the "excitement" they experience in taking risks and leaving certain things to chance.

My suggestion to these individuals would be to take that portion of your savings not earmarked for retirement income generation, and invest as aggressively as you are comfortable with. This could potentially satisfy your thirst for risk and—who knows?—you might get lucky.

As for the chance you crave, go to Las Vegas and have some fun playing your favorite games of chance and who knows, you may get lucky. I love going to Las Vegas, but I never take more than I can afford to lose.

If excitement is what you yearn for, visit your local amusement park and ride the most thrilling rides it has. Or take up skydiving. I'm also a fan of excitement, risk and chance, but only in moderation, and only in the appropriate context. I'm pretty risk-averse when it comes to anything related to financial security, both my own and that of those I advise.

A MATTER OF TIMING

Conventional wisdom has it that people who save regularly and invest prudently will enjoy a comfortable retirement. That's certainly an admirable plan.

However, if your retirement savings are in market instruments, you are on one of the rides mentioned above. If you should happen to have the misfortune of visiting this "amusement park" at the wrong time, you can run into sequence risk and jeopardize a long retirement.

To see how even the most diligent investor can fall victim to sequence risk, consider the example of big brother Bill and little sister Jill.[16] In this scenario, Bill is three years older than Jill and so he retires three years before she does.

Suppose Bill retired in 1996 and Jill followed him out of the work force in 1999. Preparing for their golden years, they each followed the guidance of a popular national radio show host who advocated investing in a "simple, low-fee, broad-market index fund." This seemed like a practical approach to Bill and Jill. With the index fund, they received participation in the overall market, and at a relatively low cost.

Bill and Jill avoid using actively managed funds because they've heard that "most actively managed funds underperform the broad market indices over the long run anyway, therefore it doesn't make much sense to incur the additional cost." I can't tell you how many times I've heard other financial professionals say this, or something very similar.

[16] These characters are fictional and their reference is for illustrative purposes only. Your actual experience will vary.

Continuing with our example, suppose that both Bill and Jill both invested substantially and regularly throughout their adult working lives and upon retirement, each had managed to amass a retirement portfolio of exactly $1 million. Their plan for retirement income generation is to follow the 4% Rule, and so they each begin their respective retirements with a $40,000 (4% of $1 million) portfolio withdrawal.

SEQUENCE RISK: TIMING IS EVERTHING

4% Initial Withdrawal Rate with 3% Inflation Adjustment

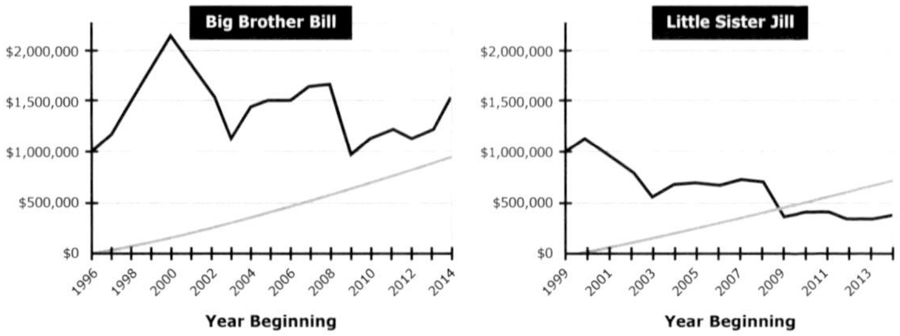

ASSUMPTIONS

- $1,000,000 - Initial Investment
- 4% Withdrawal Rate with 3% Inflation Adjustment
- $40,000 - Beginning Withdrawal Amount
- $66,114 - Ending Withdrawal Amount
- Time Period: 12/31/1995 to 12/31/2013

ENDING BALANCE

- $936,577 - Cumulative Withdrawal
- $1,545,596 - Bill's Portfolio *(+54.56% Change in Value)*

ASSUMPTIONS

- $1,000,000 - Initial Investment
- 4% Withdrawal Rate with 3% Inflation Adjustment
- $40,000 - Beginning Withdrawal Amount
- $60,504 - Ending Withdrawal Amount
- Time Period: 12/31/1998 to 12/31/2013

ENDING BALANCE

- $743,957- Cumulative Withdrawal
- $393,510 - Jill's Portfolio *(-60.65% Change in Value)*

Bill and Jill increased their withdrawals by 3% each year, as the 4% Rule calls for, in order to account for the diminishing effects of inflation on real purchasing power. Their results are shown on the two charts above, one for each of the siblings. The black line indicates their respective portfolio values over time, and the grey line demonstrates the cumulative withdrawals that each make over the same corresponding period of time. As you can see from his chart, Bill benefits fully from the market expansion of 1996 through 1999. This launches his retirement successfully.

Even though Bill then experiences two severe bear markets, from 2000-2002 and from 2008-2009, by the end of 2013, he still has more than he started with. His $1 million investment in a broad market index fund has grown to over $1.5 million in 18 years or just over halfway into his projected 30 year retirement.

In fact, Bill has been enjoying a very comfortable and relaxed retirement. He started out with a $40,000 withdrawal in 1996. By 2013, after 3% annual increases, Bill was able to withdraw over $66,000 in income from his retirement portfolio.

Now take a look at younger sister Jill's chart. Remember, in this example Jill did everything the same as her big brother. She accumulated a $1 million portfolio and invested in the same broad market index fund exactly as Bill did.

BORN TOO LATE

Jill's only "mistake" was to be born three years later, and so she retired in 1999, just before the peak of the technology boom and the subsequent economic contraction of 2000-2002.

Thus, Jill only enjoyed a single positive yearly return at the very start of her retirement and then three consecutive years of substantial losses. At this point, Jill's $1 million retirement fund was barely above $500,000, down nearly 50%, just four years into her assumed 30 year retirement.

After a few years of lateral movement, Jill's portfolio suffered heavy losses during the financial crisis of late 2008. In fact, after the losses incurred in the fourth quarter of 2008, the value of her portfolio had depreciated to well under $500,000.

Look at the performance of Jill's portfolio in the strong recovery years after the 2008 crash. With a significantly reduced base, Jill's index fund was barely keeping up with her annual withdrawals.

In fact, with yearly withdrawals of over $60,000 now, and a total portfolio value of under $400,000, Jill is now withdrawing an astonishing 15% of her entire savings. Barring an absolute miracle in the future performance of her index fund, I don't know how our friend Jill will be able to maintain her projected, inflation adjusted withdrawals for another 10 or 20 years.

LUCK OF THE DRAW

As you can see by the tale of Bill and Jill, if you base your entire retirement financial plan on the performance of the financial markets, then diligence and investment skill won't matter as much as luck. Bill and Jill did all the "right" things, to prepare for their retirement, but Bill retired at the right time and Jill retired at the wrong time.

The siblings both had the same amount to start with and stayed on the same withdrawal schedule, yet Bill has nearly four times as much money as Jill because he retired in time to benefit from four positive stock market years before a negative year, while Jill was not so fortunate. I wouldn't want to be a retiree in Jill's position now.

Why should careful, thoughtful people—the Jills of the world who retired in 1999, say, or in 2007—suffer through a financially distressing retirement? I don't think retirement success should be random, so I have developed my Income Allocation plan.

My goal with Income Allocation is to keep a Jill-like experience from happening to you; that's why I'm writing this book.

In my opinion, it's absolutely critical for retirees to

make sure their income need is met from a dependable source—dare I say, a contractually guaranteed arrangement with a financially stable company that has a long and successful history?

You may say, "If that's your plan, my retirement finances will depend on an insurance company to pay me the promised income and not go broke." That's true. Yet I'm willing to put my trust in huge, highly-rated companies that have made it through the Great Depression and the 2008 financial crisis, as well as the countless wars, recessions and inflationary periods in between. I'll take that chance with an established insurance company, rather than with the stock market.

COVERING YOUR COSTS

So far, I've explained the reasons why Income Allocation is needed in retirement and mentioned FIAs as preferred products to provide needed cash flow. How does Income Allocation work to solve the problems of longevity and sequence risk?

First, retirement income sources and annual retirement expenses should be determined. Typically these amounts are found by going through several months' worth of checking account records, credit card bills, and statements from your service providers and the financial institutions holding your assets.

Second, set a goal for retirement accumulation. Suppose retirement income needs are estimated to be $70,000 per year, while dependable income sources are $40,000. In that case, $30,000 would be the number for that first year of retirement's income needs.

Taking into account the extended longevity enjoyed by many today, along with the low interest rate environment that continues to keep yields on savings instruments depressed, I'd say that following a "3% Rule" would be more prudent than the standard 4% criteria. It would be prudent, even under a more conservative "3% Rule" assumption, to have $1,000,000 saved in order to start retirement with a $30,000 (3% of $1 million) withdrawal.

ACTION PLAN

Okay, so you have an ample amount saved for retirement. How would my Income Allocation strategy offer more security than a traditional 3% or 4% withdrawal plan?

To illustrate, I'll tell you about a recent meeting with a prospective client who is retired and is keeping his investments at a major brokerage firm. This individual (call him Craig)[17] has $1.75 million in savings; he was delaying claiming Social Security until age 70.

Now Craig is age 65, taking $7,000 per month ($84,000 a year) from his savings to meet his living costs in retirement. That $84,000 is almost 5% of his $1.75 million in savings, not the "traditional" 4% withdrawal. In addition, $1.35 million (77%) of Craig's savings is invested in equities or in other assets with some degree of market risk. The other $400,000, his "conservative money," is earning less than 1% annually in low-yield bank and money market accounts.

Just to fill in the picture, Craig's wife Donna[17] is 59 and not employed outside the home. To say that I was seeing many serious financial concerns for this couple would be an understatement.

How did I address their problems? To start, I recommended that Craig begin his Social Security benefits right away. He would receive $2,550 per month—$30,600

[17] A fictitious name has been used for privacy purposes. The experience of this individual is not intended to be representative of what your experience might be and is no guarantee of future success.

a year. By starting his Social Security benefits, Craig will reduce his savings drawdown from $84,000 a year to $53,400. With Craig's $1.75 million in savings, taking out $53,400 a year is a more reasonable 3% withdrawal rate.

SOONER RATHER THAN LATER

Starting Social Security at age 65 may seem controversial. You can delay starting until as late as age 70 and receive a benefit increase of 8% for every year you wait. Why pass up a promised 8% annual pay hike from the federal government?

Well, waiting until age 70 may be fine if you're still working and not tapping your savings to pay the bills. That wasn't the case for Craig and Donna, though. Neither has any earned income now so they're living entirely on withdrawals from savings.

You might question my judgment but I've run the numbers and I cannot make sense of spending capital and delaying Social Security. Yes, I understand that the Social Security benefit increases 8% per year, so some people argue that delaying those benefits is equal to earning 8% on that money.

Maybe this is true but I have two concerns. First, the money you withdraw from savings to get this higher future income is gone forever. You'll never see those dollars again. Second, most people have no idea how long they're going to live. A married couple can collect two Social Security checks but after the death of the first spouse, the survivor receives only one benefit.

Keeping those facts in mind, suppose a husband dies at age 71 after using over $120,000 in savings to get that higher income? His widow would then lose one Social Security benefit and her net worth would be lower by $120,000, plus whatever that $120,000 could have earned.

Therefore, I don't think tapping savings to delay Social Security works for married couples. For a single person, the question of whether to postpone Social Security is debatable, depending on how much a person has saved and how much he or she will spend.

TAKING A CHANCE

To continue with my plan for Craig, I suggested that Donna start receiving Social Security benefits in seven years, at age 66. At that point, Donna would get half of Craig's current benefit, or over $15,000 per year.

Making normal adjustments for inflation, I projected that this couple would then need almost $105,000 a year to cover their expenses while the two Social Security checks would total $55,000 a year. With those projections, Craig and Donna would need about $50,000 a year from their portfolio.

Let's look forward seven years and make some assumptions. Craig and Donna now have $1,750,000, largely in stocks and similar assets. If the market performs well, they could have over $2,000,000 despite their withdrawals. By taking $50,000 a year from their savings, they would have a modest 2.5% withdrawal rate.

However, there is no guarantee that the stock market will move higher. Suppose instead that the market corrects and is 30% lower in seven years. In the second scenario, Craig and Donna could have less than $1 million then, drawing down a risky 5% ($50,000 of $1 million) a year. Still relatively young, they would be at-risk of running short of money during retirement. I asked Craig, why leave such an important outcome to chance?

TRIPLE TIERS

Therefore, I suggested an alternative approach—my Income Allocation plan—to help Craig and Donna increase the likelihood of a successful retirement. Under this plan, they would create three different buckets of money. One bucket would be structured to meet their income needs for 8 to 10 years. The next bucket would begin paying income in 10 years, while the third bucket would contain investments with the potential for long-term growth.

For the first bucket, I suggested a specific private wealth management firm. This money manager has produced remarkable returns since 1992, with never a negative year!

Even in 2008, when most money managers had huge losses, this firm made over 7%. With its low-risk strategy, this firm had positive returns in each year of the 2000-2002 downturn as well.

With a track record like that, why not use this wealth manager for 100% of the couple's assets? The answer is that just because this firm has never had a negative year, it doesn't mean that can't happen.

As mentioned, Craig and Donna will need $50,000 a year from their portfolio. I suggested putting $400,000 of their savings into this bucket, to be managed by this excellent firm.

Remember, I mentioned that $400,000 was earning far less than 1%. My plan for this bucket was to keep these funds 100% liquid, so they could spend down that money, yet also potentially increase the rate of return. A higher return would allow Craig and Donna to squeeze a few more years of retirement cash flow from this $400,000.

Despite all the wealth management firm's prior success, I'm going to plan for a return that's three to four percentage points below this firm's compounded return over more than two decades, to build in a margin for error. Even at the lower projected return, I'm confident that Craig and Donna will get what they need from this bucket over 8 to 10 years, and probably have some money left over.

LONG-TERM TACTICS

The next bucket is our Income Allocation strategy bucket. I'm recommending Craig and Donna put part of their portfolio in a fixed index annuity (FIA) with an income rider. There are several products from some of the top-rated carriers available in the market today that would generate approximately the same income stream. In this illustration, I chose a product[18] that will guarantee them a minimum yearly income of just under $50,000 per year (starting in year 10), for as long as either is alive.

They will employ almost $600,000 of their portfolio assets to purchase the FIA in this bucket. This FIA allows for some growth on top of its contractual guarantees. Generally speaking, these products all possess similar traits that have the potential to decrease or increase the amount of the income payment the client will receive.

These distinctions can vary from carrier to carrier. Some of these features are chosen by the contract holder from the available set or range at the time the contract is written; some provide for making a selection later on, at the time you elect to begin withdrawals; still others are set by the carrier or by a condition, and not elected by the client.

Some FIAs may offer a premium bonus[19] increasing withdrawal rates based on how long you hold the product, age at purchase or age at income election; some FIAs

---

[18] As this book goes to print, there are multiple products available in the marketplace that would produce similar income streams based on the product features and benefits selected.

[19] Bonus annuities may include higher surrender charges, longer surrender periods, lower caps, higher spreads, or other restrictions that are not included in similar annuities that don't offer a premium bonus feature.

increase the income value based on index interest, joint life payments versus single life payments, payments based on a male or based on a female, etc. The variations are numerous and most will be covered later in this book.

Craig and Donna have their "floor" established with nearly $50,000 per year, beginning in 10 years. The beautiful thing here is that their "ceiling" could potentially be significantly higher. They can rest assured that their calculated income needs are covered and yet remain hopeful for more. In fact, it is feasible that the amount of their annual income from this product could be as much as $60,000 or even $70,000!

To put those numbers into perspective, suppose Craig and Donna decided instead to follow the traditional "4% Rule" for drawing down their savings. That is, they would start by withdrawing 4% of savings and increase that amount for inflation each year.

With the 4% Rule, the couple's $600,000 investment would need to grow to $1.7 million to allow such withdrawals from a sound plan. In other words, their $600,000 would need more than 170% growth in just 10 years, in order to provide the same level of income that this FIA has the potential to provide.

With something as critical as my clients' retirement income at stake, I prefer the FIA's chances of delivering the appropriate income stream. In subsequent chapters of this book you'll learn more about FIAs and the income riders that can be purchased as "add-ons" to the contract for an additional cost.

After filling the first two buckets, Craig and Donna will have $750,000 to invest for the longer term, where they can be a little more aggressive. Again, I'm going to use some excellent private wealth managers that have amazing track records.

One of my favorite managers, for example, went to a cash position (90-day Treasury bills) in November 2007, almost a year before the worst of the 2008 crash, and went out of that cash position, back into stocks, in May 2009, when the recovery had just begun. That's right, this firm missed most of the financial crisis, with a mere 1% loss in 2008 and a 38% gain in 2009. Obviously, I don't use traditional mutual funds for my client's investments. I believe in private wealth management firms that are more tactical (actively moving in and out of stocks) rather than firms that just buy and hold.

Given the track records, I've identified top private wealth managers and placed our family's savings with them. It's true that a great track record is no guarantee of superior performance during the next crisis, but I'll invest money with such firms, instead of relying upon what I've seen from the mutual fund industry. The ability to move to the safety of a cash position rather than staying in stocks and taking huge losses is very appealing to me and to my clients.

WEALTH REPLACEMENT

As you can see, I'd be using about 57% of Craig's portfolio—$1 million of $1.75 million—to meet his income need for the next ten years and beyond. Before this, he and Donna were using 100% of their savings for cash flow. Let's say bucket number three, our long-term bucket that we should not need to touch for many years, averages a 7.2% annual return, which is well below the average for the selected private wealth managers.

Then Craig and Donna would have their entire portfolio value rebuilt in about 12 years, all in addition to the $50,000 or more of annual income that is in their plan.

In other words, when Craig and Donna eventually regain their $1,750,000 in savings, this will be extra money that they don't need to generate income. If this takes the estimated 12 years, Craig will be 77 and Donna will be 71, statistically with many more years to live and enjoy their well-planned retirement.

Here's another way to look at this plan. To practically take longevity risk and sequence risk off the table for Craig and Donna, they are using less than 35% of their savings ($600,000 of $1.75 million). That's what they'll invest in an FIA, to create lifetime income that will start in 10 years.

Until then, Craig and Donna will need a financial bridge for the next 10 years. Technically, they have $1.15 million to do that. Whatever Craig and Donna have at the end of the 10 years should be "extra money," while their ongoing income needs have already been addressed by way of the cash flow generated by the FIA they purchased.

I like the triple bucket approach because specific dollars are set aside for clients' short-term income needs; for 10 years, in the case of Craig and Donna. Then the FIA cash flow will kick in, alleviating exposure to longevity risk and sequence risk.

This strategy can provide clients with the mindset and comfort level to be a bit more aggressive with the third bucket, aiming to rebuild their original savings amount as soon as possible.

Regardless of when that happens, the extra accumulation is just icing on the cake because that money won't be needed to generate income.

ALTERNATIVE APPROACH

Instead, you could implement Income Allocation with only two buckets: an FIA and the balance of your savings for the short-term bridge as well as long-term wealth rebuilding. You can solve the problems of retirement cash flow with either approach, but for Craig and Donna I suggested the three-bucket approach.

Retirees' situations may differ from each other in some details but they're basically similar. Retirees have a set amount of money that has to generate a certain amount of income for an indefinite period of time.

Usually, I find the more favorable plan is to structure the FIA to defer payments for five or seven or even 10 years. The longer the deferral, generally the higher the payout. However, the determining factor typically is the tradeoff between how much income you'll need from the FIA and how much savings will be left over after acquiring the FIA to meet that income need.

Summing up, my goal with Income Allocation is to help you meet your income needs throughout retirement using the lowest possible amount of your savings. By eliminating the need for you to use every dollar you've saved to generate retirement income, Income Allocation can actually provide funds for you to do those things you've thought about doing for a long time: buy a second home or condo, take a wonderful trip (or maybe several of them!), buy a motor home or a desirable car.

How can Income Allocation accomplish all that? Because proper implementation of Income Allocation will permit you to meet your retirement income needs with only some of your savings. The remainder of your savings can be spent on items or activities you don't really need, but really want.

Of course, I would certainly recommend investing some or most of the money left over after satisfying your income needs. Whether or not you do so, spending from this remaining amount will not deplete your income base and thereby will not put more pressure on your portfolio.

I could give you several more examples of how my clients use Income Allocation but my goal here is to introduce a concept. Hopefully you're working with a trusted financial professional who thinks the concepts in this book are viable; if so, I hope this advisor will recommend something very much along the lines of Income Allocation. Once you've covered your retirement cash flow needs with this Income Allocation plan, you can use the balance of your savings to pursue the retirement you've dreamed about.

CHAPTER THREE

WHAT HASN'T WORKED– AND WHY

As explained, Baby Boomer retirees are not likely to have the comfortable, secure retirements that their parents and grandparents enjoyed. For one reason, fewer Boomers will receive pensions; for another, many employers that promised pensions and medical coverage to retirees are trimming those costly benefits.

Indeed, retirees generally face steep uninsured health care bills these days, and that's especially true for those who need custodial care. Active retirees will find travel and recreation and dining out to be increasingly expensive while Boomers who are putting their late-in-life kids through college face soaring outlays for higher education.

In addition, life expectancy keeps increasing, so today's retirees may have to manage for 30 or 40 years without earned income, rather than the 5 or 10 years that was common when the Social Security program was launched. The bottom line is that there is a real chance Boomers will run short of money over an extended retirement.

LOWERING THE BOOMERS

The problem described above has been evident since the early years of this century, when the oldest Baby

Boomers began to retire. Some solutions have been touted, but in my opinion have some shortcomings.

Among those solutions is the strategy of "spend investment income, not principal." That might have worked well during the second half of the 20th Century, when yields on savings and investments were at moderate to high levels, but not today.

Suppose Fred Randall[20] retired in 1975 with a moderate amount of liquid assets. Fred might have put his money into bank CDs, high-quality bonds, and dividend-paying stocks. Chances are, Fred could have afforded a pleasant retirement, funded by Social Security and that investment income, as well as a pension, which many retirees received then. Fred's investment principal would have been kept intact for an emergency; assuming there was no financially devastating event, Fred's liquid assets would have passed to his loved ones eventually.

Today, such a scenario is unlikely. When Fred's granddaughter Grace[20] retires, she probably won't have a pension. She might have a sizable amount in her IRA or her 401(k), after decades of government-encouraged tax-deferred savings, but what will Grace do with her money then?

If Grace emulates her grandfather Fred and invests for investment interest in bank accounts and money market funds and bonds, she'll find yields at historically low levels. That money may be safe but Grace won't get much cash flow to spend. Even if Grace has $1 million to deposit, the amount she can expect now might be under $10,000 a year.

It's true that Grace can put money into bonds and dividend-paying stocks for slightly higher (but still relatively low) yields. However, bonds and especially stocks can lose value, eroding Grace's principal, while she also faces the risk that a weak economy can bring reductions in stock dividends. If Grace wants really protected money

[20] These characters are fictional and their reference is for illustrative purposes only. Your actual experience will vary.

from familiar vehicles, she'll have to accept little or no investment income as well.

DIPPING INTO PRINCIPAL

Thus, the traditional spend-income-but-preserve-principal strategy won't suffice for most retiring Boomers, because of low savings yields and the lack of pensions. For a comfortable retirement, it probably will be necessary to spend down investment principal.

Again, there's a traditional method: the immediate annuity. With this type of annuity, also called an income annuity, you give money to an insurance company and get cash flow right away.

If you wish, you can arrange for the cash to keep flowing for as long as you live. A married couple can get a joint annuity that will continue to pay out as long as either spouse is alive, no matter how many years that might be.

An immediate annuity can offer a means of swapping savings for income that's guaranteed to last a lifetime, with no time limit.

However, immediate annuities aren't always so popular with Boomers (or dare I say with anyone else, for that matter). For one thing, low interest rates are reflected in low annuity payouts. A couple retiring in their 60s might receive only $5,000 or $6,000 a year from a $100,000 investment, depending on the product features they choose.

Immediate annuity payouts usually are fixed, so buyers lose spending power over time. If you want some inflation adjustment to keep up with the cost of living, you'll have to start with an even lower amount of cash flow.

In addition, people generally don't like the loss of liquidity with some products and the idea that with some products nothing will go to heirs if they die after receiving few annuity payments.

Despite a generally negative outlook on immediate annuities among consumers and advisors, they may offer benefits to certain buyers. At a time when investment yields are relatively low, a 65-year-old paying $100,000 for a lifetime annuity might get $650 a month. (That's a hypothetical amount, reflecting current payouts on some annuities, with certain features.) A $650 monthly payout equals $7,800 a year, for a 7.8% percentage payout on a $100,000 outlay.

Now, 7.8% is much higher than today's investment yields. Insurers may be able to offer that much, or a payout somewhere in that neighborhood, because the 7.8% payout is composed of three forms of cash flow. One flow is a return of the $100,000 principal, in this example. With a traditional lifetime annuity, the amount you pay won't be returned, so you're essentially getting a return of your principal over your projected life expectancy. (Immediate annuities often offer some beneficiary payments, but these require a reduction in monthly cash flow.)

Besides a return of principal, the second cash flow is the interest rate you receive on your purchase, just as you receive interest on a bond or a bank account. In today's environment, that rate is relatively low.

The third income stream of an immediate annuity, boosting the payout percentage, comes from "longevity credits," also called "mortality credits." Here, the insurer adds a bit to the promised payments to account for the presumed early death of some immediate annuity buyers.

As a simple example, assume that five seniors take an annual golfing trip; each year they fund the next year's outing. In our scenario, each one puts $1,000 into a shoe box and they tape the box shut. Now they know that future trips will be funded.

Because they're getting older, these five seniors have an agreement: if one of them dies, the other four can spend the money in the shoebox. Suppose that one year later, one of the friends has died. The four remaining golfers open the shoebox and discover that there's still $5,000 in there. The money didn't grow by one penny but now the four survivors each can spend $1,250, if they choose. They each received a 25% return—from a $1,000 outlay to $1,250 available—which is a mortality credit, due to one contributor's death.

Say they decide not to take the trip and they tape the box shut, leaving the money for the next year with the same agreement. Again, one of the group dies. When the three remaining golfers open the box there is still $5,000 in there. Therefore, each of them has just under $1,700 to spend, so they have realized almost a 67% rate of return (from $1,000 to nearly $1,700) in two years, even though the money hasn't grown. And so on.

This is an example of a mortality credit because those who die early fund those who live longer. Only an insurance company can do this, and it explains why immediate annuity payouts may be appealing, to some people in some circumstances.

ASSESSING ASSET ALLOCATION

If immediate annuities aren't always the best answer, retiring Boomers must find another way to turn their savings and investments into a lifelong stream of secure, ample cash flow. Some advisors have advocated asset allocation, also known as modern portfolio theory. The idea behind this theory is that all investments can be grouped into certain asset classes. Stocks (or equities) are considered an asset class.

To distinguish between shares in Microsoft and shares

in a new fast food chain, the equity asset class might be divided into large-caps (for market capitalization, the value of the outstanding shares), mid-caps and small-caps. Other stock market sub-categories can be identified. Bonds (known as fixed income), real estate, commodities, and precious metals (primarily gold) also may be considered asset classes. Other asset classes might be included, depending on who is keeping count.

Proponents of asset allocation believe that investors should hold a mix of these asset classes, for successful long-term results.

You can build a portfolio this way while you're working and have earned income to invest; then you can gradually re-shape your portfolio, spending down your assets to provide retirement income.

When you strip away the bells and whistles, the main tenet of asset allocation is that investors should hold some combination of high-potential assets, mainly stocks, and some lower-risk assets, mainly bonds. Various asset classes aren't "correlated," so they won't all move in the same direction at the same time. Thus, investors might get high long-term returns from stocks while their bonds will act to dampen overall portfolio volatility. Long-term, the right mix will produce an acceptable level of growth as well as tolerable downturns when stocks hit a rough patch.

That was the theory, but asset allocation has failed in this century. In 2000-2002 and again in 2008-2009, stocks tumbled sharply, depriving investors of huge amounts of lifetime savings.

Those were the times when "safe" assets such as bonds were supposed to act as stabilizers. However, bonds failed to produce the desired results, especially in the financial crisis of 2008-2009.

When stocks crashed then, all the supposedly "non-correlated" assets went down with them. Real estate went down. Gold went down. Stocks from all over the world plunged with the U.S. equities market.

The same was true with the bonds and bond funds that were supposed to be the safe portion of investors' portfolios. Even short-term bond funds lost heavily. Indeed, investors in some of these funds were dismayed to discover what low-quality holdings were in the funds, in some cases delivering losses that exceeded the setbacks of the broad U.S. stock market.

Thus, we've learned that bonds aren't safe investments for retirees desiring principal stability. "Fixed income" investments can't guarantee stable prices.

If you want true protection from market risks as well as income for your retirement, you should move beyond asset allocation to a concept I call "Income Allocation." First, though, I want to cover a little more in-depth a retirement income practice that has evolved from asset allocation—the 4% Rule—and explain why that approach, too, can leave retiring Baby Boomers short of cash flow in the future.

BREAKING THE RULE

The so-called 4% Rule starts with asset allocation. That is, investors are assumed to start their retirement years with a certain portfolio allocation. Often it's a 50-50 or a 60-40 split between various types of stocks and various types of bonds. It's usually assumed that retirees maintain that allocation throughout their remaining years.

From there, advisors who recommend the 4% Rule tell their clients to start their retirement by spending 4% of their portfolio assets in Year One. In subsequent years, the portfolio withdrawals can increase with the cost of living. Judging by historic investment results, this method has a high probability of avoiding portfolio depletion over a 30-year retirement. In effect, the 4% Rule is designed to help investors create a synthetic pension with money they've saved while working. Earlier, we saw that Fred Randall retired with a modest amount of savings in 1975; he used the investment income from those savings as well as his pension and his Social Security benefits to fund a long, comfortable retirement.

Now suppose that Fred's granddaughter Grace plans to retire soon. She won't have a pension from her employer but she does expect to have $1 million in her 401(k) account from her salary deferrals, employer matching contributions, and investment gains inside the plan.

At retirement, Grace will roll her 401(k) money into an IRA. If she has $1 million then, she can withdraw $40,000 (4% of her $1 million IRA) for spending money in the first year. If inflation is 3% that year, Grace will increase her withdrawal by 3%, to $41,200, in the second year. And so on, year after year. Her $40,000 of annual withdrawals will grow to $45,000, $50,000, and even higher, maintaining her lifestyle for 30 years, according to advisors who support the 4% Rule.

Following the 4% Rule allows Grace to use her portfolio to get cash flow year after year, expected to last for 30 years. What's more, this synthetic pension is indexed to inflation. Grace still has full control of her assets, which she can access if necessary, or leave to loved ones, which would not be the case with a traditional pension or an immediate annuity.

All in all, the 4% Rule sounds good, and many advisors put their clients on this path. Yet doubts have arisen. Articles such as, "The 4 Percent Rule is Not Safe in a Low-Yield World," by researchers from Texas Tech University, the American College, and Morningstar Investment Management have raised doubts about this process.[21]

This article concludes that today's low-yield environment "causes the projected failure rate for retirement account withdrawals to jump to 57%." That is,

---

[21] Finke, Michael, Wade D. Pfau, and David M. Blanchett. 2013. "The 4 Percent Rule Is Not Safe in a Low-Yield World." Journal of Financial Planning 26 (6): 46–55.

low bond yields can decrease a portfolio's growth and lead to faster depletion. Instead of a 4% initial withdrawal, the "safe" initial withdrawal rate might be 3% or less.

Think about the above number—57% is the projected failure rate! Now, imagine getting on an airplane that has only a 43% chance to make it to its intended destination safely. I can envision an empty airplane! Yet there are millions of people following a strategy that a study from three very credible sources says has up to a 57% failure rate. This to me is unbelievable.

Just as low bond yields can imperil a retirement based on the 4% Rule, the same can be said for stock market volatility. If there is a steep downturn in the early years of a retirement, the chances of running out of money increase dramatically.

An article titled, "Say Goodbye To The 4% Rule," published in the Wall Street Journal, made this point by saying that "the 4% rule has been thrown into doubt, thanks to an unexpected hazard: the risk of a prolonged market rout the first two, or even three years of your retirement." In such an event, "the danger of running out of money increases."[22]

To see how this might look, go back to the above example. Grace withdraws $40,000 from her $1 million portfolio in Year 1 of retirement and $41,200 in Year 2, adjusting for inflation. With another year of 3% inflation, Grace would be withdrawing about $42,500 in Year 3.

However, what will happen if a stock market crash drops the value of Grace's IRA from $1 million to, say, $700,000?

Continuing with a $42,500 distribution would raise the withdrawal rate to more than 6%, which would hasten depletion.

If Grace wants to continue with a "safe" distribution plan, she'd have to take much less spending money from her portfolio. You can start your retirement by using the

[22] Greene, Kelly. "Say Goodbye to the 4% Rule." WSJ. Dow Jones & Company, Inc., 03 Mar. 2013. Web. 29 Dec. 2014.

4% Rule but there are no guarantees that you'll be able to keep withdrawing the planned cash flow.

In addition, the 4% Rule is by no means simple to implement. Suppose Grace's $1 million IRA produces $20,000 (2%) a year in dividends and investment interest, which she'll withdraw.

If she wants to distribute $41,200 in Year 2 of her retirement, Grace will have to sell $21,200 of her portfolio assets to find the cash. Which stocks should she sell? Which bonds? Grace or her advisors must make such decisions every year, and there is no certainty these decisions will be correct 100% of the time.

Aside from the above, a 4% initial distribution rate isn't that exciting. After saving and investing enough to build up a $1 million IRA, Grace may not be pleased to learn she can use only $40,000 of that account to help her enjoy her new retirement.

For all of the above reasons, the 4% Rule can lead to unhappy results. Even William Bengen, the financial planner who is known as the creator of this rule, has since advised caution.

When asked whether he followed the 4% Rule in his own retirement, Bengen replied, "I wouldn't do it." As Bengen put it, following this rule "is probably not wise—even dangerous—because there are very simple assumptions that I used to develop that rule."[23] So Bengen won't trust it for his own retirement, but millions have been advised that it is a viable strategy? Again, to me this is unbelievable.

Sadly, many people have taken the 4% Rule and asset allocation theories as facts, not opinions. Those retirees who were also negatively affected by investment results from 2000-2010 will likely be dealing with the failings of these beliefs for many years to come.

If the 4% Rule and asset allocation principles are

[23] Here & Now: "Rethinking The 4 Percent Rule For Retirement." 90.9 wbur Boston's NPR® News Station, 29 November 2013. http://hereandnow.wbur.org/2013/11/29/four-percent-rule

dangerous, why follow them? Maybe it's time to consider an Income Allocation strategy that's based on money you can rely upon to cover your living expenses in retirement.

I would now like to present the finer details of the method I use to help protect my clients' retirement assets.

CHAPTER FOUR

FOCUSING ON FIXED INDEX ANNUITIES

Earlier, you learned about the 4% Rule and some of its shortcomings. Other rules have shortcomings as well.

For example, the "Rule of 100" has been a handy way to construct investment portfolios. Under this rule, you take someone's age and subtract it from 100. The answer is the desired allocation to equities.

Thus, someone who retires at age 65 would have an allocation of 35% in stocks and 65% in bonds. At 85, that retiree would have only 15% in stocks and the balance in supposedly safe, income-producing bonds.

Recently, some commentators have suggested tweaking the rule to reflect longer life expectancy. With a Rule of, say, 110 that 65-year-old would have a 45% allocation to stocks, not 35%. With a Rule of 120, that 65-year-old would have 55% in stocks. The more stocks, the greater the potential for ongoing growth over a long retirement.

FINDING THE FLAWS

Now, there's nothing wrong with a substantial allocation to equities in retirement. Yes, stocks are volatile but well-chosen stocks have been long-term winners.

The problem lies on the other side of these Rules, which all recommend increasing allocations to bonds. As we've seen, today's bonds and bond funds won't deliver safety or adequate income to retirees.

When stocks fall, bonds are likely to tumble with them. Current interest rates translate into low yields. Moreover, if interest rates rise from today's levels—as they will, at some time in the future—the value of an investor's bonds will decline.

INTRODUCING INCOME ALLOCATION

My response to these Rules is to look at them from a different perspective. As a result, I've come to favor another concept: Income Allocation. The idea is to devote enough money to a vehicle that delivers guaranteed income; the balance of a portfolio can be invested in stocks or other assets with growth potential.

Previously, I described my plan for Adam and Beth Walker,[24] who are 61 and 59 years old. They expect to retire in about five years, and they calculate a need for $40,000 a year—on top of their Social Security benefits—to cover their living expenses.

Currently, the Walkers have $1 million in investable assets. I advised them to place half of those assets—$500,000—into a product that promises them about $36,000 a year, for the rest of their lives. To get that amount, they will have to wait to start collecting for five years, until they retire.

What's more, that $36,000 is the minimum amount the Walkers can expect. With modest success, the Walkers will get $40,000 or more each year while either spouse is alive. Their living expenses are covered, no matter what happens in the financial markets or how long they live.

After making this $500,000 commitment, the Walkers have another $500,000 in liquid assets, from their original

[24] Fictitious names have been used for privacy purposes. The experiences of these individuals is not intended to be representative of what your experience might be and is no guarantee of future success.

$1 million. They can spend that money, keep it invested for more growth, or mentally set it aside for an inheritance their children eventually will receive.

What is this product that has helped simplify life for the Walkers and the lives of so many other retiring Baby Boomers? It's the fixed index annuity (FIA) and when purchased with an optional income rider,[25] it becomes the best means I know of, for securing the guaranteed retirement income stream you need, and for as long as you live. The income rider is the secret to the promised future income.

Few people understand how these riders truly work, why they should be used, or when they should not be used. After almost 20 years of experience in dealing with these products, I feel that I've learned when and when not to use them for my clients. From here, I'll explain my Income Allocation strategy and how an FIA can make it work.

WHAT'S YOUR NUMBER?

In recent years, some major financial firms have run advertising campaigns with a "What's Your Number" theme. Alice might have a number of $450,000, Bob's number could be $700,000, and Carol might have a number of $1.3 million, and so on.

The number, as you might have guessed, refers to their savings goal. That is, when each individual manages to accumulate that number in their bank and investment accounts, he or she will be able to retire and live comfortably, without any earned income.

From my experience, most people don't realize what such numbers mean. Why should Alice be able to retire with $450,000 while Carol needs $1.3 million? And how do you calculate such a number in the first place, if it can

[25] Income benefit riders are generally optional and available for additional cost.

vary so much from one person to another?

The answer to the first question is fairly straightforward. The amount that you save and invest during your working years is meant to generate income when you retire; individual circumstances (age, health, and lifestyle) will dictate how much you need: how large is your number?

Once you understand that, you can calculate your own number. Generally, people spend about as much in retirement as they did while working. If Adam and Beth Walker spend $100,000 a year now, their retirement goal probably would be having enough income to spend $100,000 a year.

Let's say that this couple expects to receive a total of $60,000 a year from their Social Security benefits and Beth's pension from her years as a teacher. In this scenario, they would need $40,000 a year from their retirement fund. From there, the 4% Rule, explained above, makes the calculation easy: simply multiply the needed income by 25. If Alice needs $18,000 a year from her portfolio to live well in retirement, multiply $18,000 by 25 to find that her number is $450,000; if Alice needs $52,000 a year from her retirement fund, multiply $52,000 by 25 to get $1.3 million. And so on.

However, as I mentioned earlier, the 4% Rule is deeply flawed. When someone follows that rule, a financially successful retirement is too dependent on investment results for people to rely upon. Retirees (or their advisors) must constantly make the right decisions about how much money to withdraw each year and which portfolio assets to liquidate to raise the needed cash.

Just as no one knows how well financial markets will do over a 20- or 30- or 40-year retirement, no one can make all the right decisions, all the time. In a majority of cases, following the 4% Rule will result in overspending and running short of money. Just remember this one important fact: as explained previously, the man who created the 4% theory in the 1990s now doubts its viability, saying that it's dangerous to follow.

AGE-OLD CONCERNS

Will retirements really last 20 or 30 or 40 years? It is certainly possible. Today, many Americans retire right around age 65.

In 2014, the Society of Actuaries raised its life expectancy projections.[26] Now the average 65-year-old U.S. woman is expected to reach 88.8 years, up from a projection of 86.4 years in 2000. At age 65, American men are expected to reach 86.6 years, up from 84.6 years in 2000.

As the numbers indicate, today's "average" 65-year-old is expected to live on average another 20-25 years, and those numbers continue to rise. A person who has access to high quality medical care and who has lived a reasonably healthy lifestyle might anticipate living even longer, conceivably many years longer.

That's good news. The downside to living longer is that longevity leverages one's financial risks, particularly in retirement. The longer you live (you or your surviving spouse, if you're married), the greater the likelihood of encountering shortfalls in your retirement finances.

Say Tom Jones[27] retires at 65 with $500,000 in savings and investments. He spends $50,000 (10%) of that money each year. Under those circumstances, if Tom lives much past his 75th birthday, he will have outlived his resources. The same concept holds for a 5% or a 4% drawdown rate. If you are retired, say, for 30 years, there is certainly a possibility that you will encounter a financial shortfall.

[26] Society of Actuaries. Mortality Tables Report. Rep. no. RP-2014. Schaumburg: Society of Actuaries, 2014. Oct. 2014. Web. 29 Dec. 2014.

[27] This character is fictional and his reference is for illustrative purposes only. Your actual experience will vary.

Circling back to sequence risk, suppose Sue Adams[28] retired in 2007, just prior to the significant downturn of 2008-2009. The timing of Sue's retirement wouldn't matter nearly as much should she pass on in the early years of that retirement. If she does not, however, she will undoubtedly feel the substantial effects of the early-on bear market once she is 15 to 20 years into retirement, having taken her annual income withdrawals from her portfolio in each of those years.

You can add declining health to the list of risks that advance with age. The older you get, the greater the likelihood that you'll face having to spend money on expensive full-time care.

Married couples should consider the "widow's penalty" as well. After one spouse dies, the survivor usually files tax returns as a single individual—where the effective income tax rates are much higher than they are for married couples who file joint returns.

The bottom line is that as life expectancies increase, you can reasonably expect to have a prolonged retirement. That extended period of time without a paycheck can sap your resources. Therefore, a sound financial plan for retirement should include a provision for providing the necessary income—one that will cover your basic living expenses—no matter how long you live.

SECRET OF SUCCESS

Thus, the key to a financially successful retirement is to find enough predictable income (in addition to Social Security and possibly a pension) to cover your anticipated expenses, no matter how long you live. That's the idea behind "Income Allocation." If you don't have a lush pension, where can you obtain such income these days?

[28] This character is fictional and her reference is for illustrative purposes only. Your actual experience will vary.

The first clue can be found in that Wall Street Journal article mentioned above, "Say Goodbye to the 4% Rule." The author reports the results of over 200 Monte Carlo computer simulations: "...assuming returns based on current market conditions, the winning combination turns out to be a 50/50 mix of stocks and fixed annuities."

Okay, half the portfolio goes into stocks, for long-term growth, despite the volatility that you'll have to live with. While the other half of your money goes into...fixed annuities?

DEFINING THE TERMS

An *annuity* offers a regular stream of payments. You can purchase a lifetime annuity, guaranteed by the financial strength and claims paying ability of the insurance company, to last as long as you live or, if you're married, as long as either you or your spouse is alive.

Annuities can be either *fixed* or *variable*. Brokerage firms are often partial to variable annuities, mainly because of the securities component of these products.

Variable annuities may well be suitable for some, but they don't fit well with my Income Allocation strategy. As the name indicates, variable annuities can deliver varying results. Typically, variable annuities are heavily invested in equity markets. Values can go up...but they also can go down.

My Income Allocation strategy calls for the use of vehicles that are not dependent on any market to provide dependable cash flow; variable annuities are too...well... variable to provide reliable, substantial income.

Fixed annuities, on the other hand, build value with much less variability. The *Wall Street Journal* article has a quote from a professor who studies retirement income: "'There is no need for retirees to hold bonds,' he says. Instead, annuities, with their promise of income for life, act like 'super bonds with no maturity dates.'"

The article doesn't spell out what type of fixed annuities were used in the computer simulations. However, the next paragraph in the article goes on to describe immediate annuities, so it's apparent those are the annuities that were in the computer simulations. With an immediate annuity, you pay cash to an insurance company and receive a stream of payments that begins right away. As I mentioned above—and as the *Wall Street Journal* article points out—immediate annuities have flaws. Generally, there's no access to your money, once the payments begin.

In addition, immediate annuities typically have fixed payouts, so they won't help address inflation. What's more, if you purchase an immediate annuity now, the payments likely will be scant because you will be locking in today's low savings yields for the rest of your life.

BETTER LATER THAN SOONER

If immediate fixed annuities have drawbacks, where can you turn? The alternative is to own a deferred fixed annuity. Here, you buy now and watch your money potentially grow inside the annuity contract, free of income tax.

You wait for a while—perhaps many years—before starting an annuity income stream. Meanwhile, you have some access to the money you've put into this product. If your contract value grows, the amount of cash you can pull from the annuity contract also can grow, so there is some potential inflation protection as well.

You might, for instance, put money into a CD that would guarantee an X% annual return for, say, five years. After that five years, you could renew the CD at the rate then being offered, or you could cash in the CD and take it to a different bank. In the same way, fixed annuities offer a minimum fixed rate of return for a certain time period—for simplicity, we'll call it five years. At the end of that 5-year term, you can keep the fixed annuity or cash it in and use the money to purchase a different annuity from another insurance company offering more favorable terms, such as a higher yield. Keep in mind that any distributions may be subject to ordinary income tax and, if taken prior to age 59½, an additional 10% federal tax.

Unfortunately, today's low interest rates are reflected in the yields of traditional deferred fixed annuities. Just as is the case with bank CDs, you'll lock in a low return by purchasing a traditional deferred fixed annuity today.

An alternative to a deferred fixed annuity has gained popularity: the deferred fixed index annuity (FIA). FIAs have the features of a traditional deferred fixed annuity: protection against loss due to market volatility and the ability to provide lifelong cash flow.

Moreover, by being tied to one or more financial market indexes, you'll also have the potential for substantially higher interest than you'd get in a traditional deferred fixed annuity.

If you're looking for crucial income over a long retirement, even small increases in a financial product can make a big difference. One investment "rule" that no one can question is the Rule of 72. To see how long it takes for money to double, divide the rate of return into 72. Thus, if you are earning 3% with a traditional deferred fixed annuity, it will take about 24 years for your money to double. Boost that rate to 4% and your money will double in 18 years.

Consequently, if you can find a conservative financial product that will pay you 6% a year, long-term, you'll see your money double in about 12 years. Over a 24-year retirement, your money would quadruple, with that 6% annualized return.

There's no guarantee that you'll earn 6% or even 4% a year with an FIA. However, the better FIAs are structured to increase the chance of higher long-term earnings, as compared to what you'll get with a traditional deferred fixed annuity.

CHAPTER FIVE

PUTTING INCOME FIRST

As of this writing, FIA sales are increasing by nearly 25% a year; in the third quarter of 2015 alone, total sales topped $14.4 billion, far above the previous record.[29] While it's true that FIAs are growing rapidly in popularity, it's not accurate to say that FIAs are new—I first recommended FIAs to clients almost 20 years ago, back in the mid-1990s.

FIAs may not be new, but they have a new look: they usually offer income riders.[30] As I'll explain, that's what makes FIAs the ideal financial product for an Income Allocation strategy.

FIRST THINGS FIRST

You can see the origins of today's FIAs in the first product I presented to clients. It was known as a "seven-year high water mark annuity with a 2.75% annual spread." This example illustrates what that meant:

Suppose than Jack Long[31] placed $100,000 in this annuity on June 14, 1995, when the S&P 500® Index of U.S. stocks closed at 536. This FIA called for the annuity value to be possibly increased on that anniversary date (June 14), each year for the next seven years, depending on the value of the S&P 500® then.

As it turned out, the highest point reached on those dates (the "high water mark") occurred in 1999. That was

[29] "Indexed Annuities Have Record-Breaking 3Q." InsuranceNewsNet.com, 19 November 2015. http://insurancenewsnet.com/oarticle/2015/11/19/indexed-annuities-have-record-breaking-3q.html

[30] Income benefit riders are generally optional and available at an additional cost.

[31] A fictitious name has been used for privacy purposes. The experiences of this individual is not intended to be representative of what your experience might be and is no guarantee of future success.

near the peak of the tech stock boom and just before the market crashed in the year 2000.

On June 14, 1999, the S&P 500® closed at 1,294: a gain of 142% from its 536 value at the purchase date. Then the bull market ended, stocks fell, and the S&P 500® was lower on the next three anniversary dates. By the end of the seven-year period, on June 14, 2002, the S&P 500® was down to 1,020. No matter. Jack's high water mark annuity didn't lose ground, under the contract terms. It retained its value from the June 14, 1999, peak anniversary date.

Thus, Jack's annuity was treated as having retained its 142% gain from the first four years, with no subsequent losses. That 142% gain was equal to a compound annualized return of 13.5% a year, for seven years. Then the spread (2.75% a year) was deducted, so Jack's gain for the period was calculated at 10.75% per year—13.5% minus 2.75%—for seven years. At a 10.75% annualized rate of return for seven years, Jack's $100,000 purchase of this FIA would have increased to over $200,000.

Note that Jack's annuity value more than doubled in this seven year period, even though the S&P 500® didn't even double, going from 536 on the purchase date to 1020 on the seventh anniversary date. That's because this annuity registered all the anniversary date index value increases, up to 1999, but did not penalize Jack for the losses in the subsequent bear market from 2000 to 2002.

LIMITING LOSSES

There is a truism in a retirement portfolio that is invested in the financial markets: after any loss, you need a larger gain just to break even. If you lose 10%, for example, you need an 11% gain to make up the lost ground. Lose 25% and you must gain 33.3% for a break-even; after a 50% loss, you'll need a 100% gain.

An FIA typically eliminates the possibility of a loss, so that a large break-even isn't necessary. (Some FIAs expose consumers to losses, but generally those are limited to multi-year contracts and only apply to the interest increase that have yet to be credited. I know of no FIA that subjects principal or prior credited interest to contract value loss.)

There is a tradeoff, because FIAs often have some restriction on how much the contract can grow, but the loss protection is extremely valuable.

Imagine how you would have felt, going through the 2000-2002 and 2008-2009 bear markets without any loss—and with your rise in contract value from the previous positive index performance intact! That's exactly what the experience has been for my clients who purchased FIAs: they've grown with bull markets and then gone through bear markets without losing a penny.

It's true that FIAs have changed in the past 20 years, and today's low interest rates certainly have affected product design. Nevertheless, the basics remain in place.

Once you purchase an FIA, all gains inside the annuity contract are untaxed. There is typically no limit to the amount you can put in a contract and there are no stealth taxes—that is, you don't lose tax breaks or owe more tax if your income goes over a certain amount.

With an FIA, gains in your contract value aren't really fixed, as they are with a traditional 3%-per-year-for-five-years deferred fixed annuity. Also, FIA returns are not really variable, as they are with a variable annuity that might suffer a 20% or 30% annual loss.

Instead, the gain in an FIA—known as the crediting rate—is fixed within a certain range. That range might be from zero, if a stock market index has a loss over a 12-month period, up to 70% of that market index's gain for that period. That's just one example. FIAs have many types of crediting techniques, as I'll explain later, but they generally limit losses while offering the chance for growth similar to what you'll get from bonds and potentially more than bank accounts. This upside-without-the-downside structure makes it possible for you to enjoy significant long-term growth from a high-quality FIA.

CASHING IN

Say a hypothetical Marie Knox[32] invests $50,000 in an FIA. Over the years, her FIA's value grows to $55,000, $60,000, $75,000, etc. Once Marie retires and needs the cash flow, how can she get her money out?

One way is to "annuitize" the contract, which means using the account value to obtain an immediate annuity. If Marie's account value is, say, $80,000, she can annuitize it and receive cash flow for the rest of her life, based on the amount she'd receive from an $80,000 outlay.

What's more, the annuity payments to Marie will be treated as only partially taxable and partially a tax-free return of principal. If Marie has a 25-year life expectancy when the annuity begins, for instance, and her principal was $50,000, her annual annuity payments will include $2,000 of untaxed cash flow for the first 25 years, while the rest will be taxable.

However, many people don't want to annuitize their FIAs, for the reasons mentioned above. Annuity payments are locked in, usually with no chance for growth, and annuitants (people receiving annuitized payments) typically have no access to the underlying principal.

The alternative to annuitizing is to take free withdrawals or use optional guaranteed lifetime withdrawal benefits that may be available for an additional cost from the annuity. Marie, with her $80,000 contract value, might simply withdraw $5,000 a year for living expenses in retirement.

With this approach, the money remaining in her deferred annuity can continue to grow. What's more, if Marie needs money she can withdraw some or even all of her account value.

[32] This character is fictional and her reference is for illustrative purposes only. Your actual experience will vary.

RIDING HIGH

In recent years, FIA issuers have made the choice to take withdrawals more appealing. Most FIAs now offer income riders,[33] for an extra annual fee. These riders give consumers the ability to withdraw certain amounts for the rest of their lives, no matter how long they live and regardless of how the relevant market indexes perform.

Here's an example of such a rider. Paul Randall[34] invests $100,000 in an FIA with an accumulation value that's pegged to one or more of the growth strategies explained in the following pages. Paul also purchases an income rider to that annuity with a "7.2% internal rollup;" this income rider contains a minimum withdrawal benefit when it takes effect, which usually takes several years.

With this arrangement, Paul's FIA is on two tracks. One can be called the accumulation side, pegged to one or more stock market indexes. There is upside potential there, with limited or no downside.

The other track is the income side, backed by the annuity rider. This side offers ongoing income, no matter how the market indexes perform.

Suppose Paul purchases this contract at age 55. Ten years later, the accumulation side has grown from $100,000 to $150,000, in this hypothetical example. That's Paul's money, which he can withdraw or remain in the contract or exchange for another annuity.

Regardless, Paul's income value will have grown by 7.2% a year, under the annuity rider's 7.2% internal roll-up. As you can easily tell from the Rule of 72, his $100,000 will double in those 10 years, to $200,000. That's the number Paul can use for minimum withdrawals during his lifetime, in this hypothetical illustration.

---

[33] Income benefit riders are generally optional and available at an additional cost.

[34] This character is fictional and his reference is for illustrative purposes only. Your actual experience will vary.

The amount that Paul can withdraw will depend on his age then, and on whether he wants the promised withdrawals for himself only or for his wife Sharon as well. Starting at age 65, Paul might be able to withdraw $11,000 per year (5.5% of his $200,000 income value) for as long as he lives. Alternatively, if he chooses a joint annuity, Paul and Sharon might be guaranteed $10,000 a year (5% of the $200,000 income value) for as long as either is alive.

Note that either 5% (joint) or 5.5% (single life) is better than withdrawing 4% a year under the 4% Rule. Moreover, that 5% or 5.5% is a contractual guarantee, not subject to market risk. On the other hand, that $10,000 or $11,000 a year will be fixed, for their lifetimes. There will be no appreciation potential, so Paul should think of this cash flow as the money he'll use for retirement expenses. He'll have to invest other funds elsewhere for growth and inflation protection.

However, a few companies offer annuity riders with an increasing income option. You'll start lower but the payout will increase over time. Increasing at 3% a year, for example, an $8,000 or $9,000 annual payout will become $16,000 or $18,000 in 24 years (remember the Rule of 72!), so your annuity income would increase over a long retirement.

A select few insurance companies tie your income increases to market index-linked growth, which brings you the certainty of knowing your income won't decrease, while permitting higher-than-average increases if the indexes move up. Such FIAs provide you with a way to combat future inflation.

To put this income rider into perspective, suppose that Paul purchases a $100,000 FIA at age 55 and wants to retire at 65. Then he'll start to receive $10,000 a year, for as long as either he or Sharon is alive. If Paul wanted to invest in the financial markets and follow that 4% Rule, his $100,000 would have to grow to $250,000 in 10 years: then he could withdraw $10,000 (4% of $250,000) in the year he retires, as explained in an earlier example.

Can $100,000 grow to $250,000 in 10 years? It could, but it's not a certainty. Paul would have to invest largely or entirely in stocks, to have a chance for that kind of return, and thus he would be exposed to stock market risk.

Now, investing in stocks is fine, even in retirement. Long term, results have been excellent. In fact, I'm sure you've had some broker or advisor tell you that stocks have gained 10% a year for the past century; I've certainly seen and heard those numbers.

Here's the challenge: I've yet to meet someone who has been retired for 100 years, or even 50 years for that matter! Retirement, as I mentioned earlier, can last for 30 or 40 years. Starting off with a flat stock market such as the one that lasted from 2000 to 2012 can be devastating if you're drawing down your retirement fund during a time like that.

On the other hand, if you retire at a time like 1982 and ride that type of bull market, you'll probably have no worries. The bottom line is that relying heavily on stocks means that your retirement lifestyle will be very much dependent on the first 5 to 10 years of the market's performance once you stop working. That's known as "Sequence Risk," and you can find examples throughout this text.

However, a portfolio that's heavily invested in equities is by no means housekeeping money. My Income Allocation plan starts with FIAs to provide the cash flow that you need to pay your bills for as long as you live. Think of this source of reliable income as the foundation of a house. Planning for your income needs in retirement is so critical, in my opinion, that it should be as rock solid as possible—as secure as the foundation of the dream home you would build. If the foundation is faulty, then everything built on top of it is faulty as well.

Once you know that your foundation is sound, with an FIA, you can use other funds to hold stocks and other growth opportunities. This assurance of lifelong income, combined with market-based (but not directly linked) upside potential, makes an FIA a bedrock vehicle with potentially substantial returns—an ideal fit for my Income Allocation strategy. FIA income riders usually are structured so that consumers won't owe surrender charges if they withdraw the permitted amount. However, all annuity withdrawals generally are taxable, up to the amount of earnings in the contract, and a 10% tax penalty probably will apply before age 59½.

Thus, you probably should avoid FIA withdrawals before age 59½: these annuities really are meant for retirement cash flow. Even if you sidestep the early distribution withdrawal penalty, FIA withdrawals are usually fully taxable.

Taxes may not be inevitable though, because you never have required withdrawals from an FIA that's held in a taxable account (that is, not in an IRA or another tax-favored retirement plan). If you hold an FIA in a taxable account and you don't need the money you can cut back or avoid annuity withdrawals altogether, so you won't pay taxes for money you don't really want.

CIRCLING BACK

Now that you know the basics of FIAs, we can revisit my plan for Adam and Beth Walker.[35] As mentioned, they intend to begin the transition to retirement in five years, first with Adam and then with Beth a short time later. At that point, the Walkers will need approximately $40,000 per year from their portfolio to maintain their lifestyle once the paychecks stop upon Beth's retirement.

[35] Fictitious names have been used for privacy purposes. The experiences of these individuals is not intended to be representative of what your experience might be and is no guarantee of future success.

To produce that $40,000 a year—and perhaps more—the Walkers purchased an FIA. As part of my plan, the Walkers have used only 50% of their savings to acquire an FIA that can meet their goal. This is the secret to Income Allocation, and it explains why I like this strategy so much in today's low yield, high volatility world.

One vital feature of an FIA is its ability to provide increasing amounts of cash flow over a long term if the underlying index meets certain performance criteria. When evaluating an FIA, therefore, you should take a close look at how the account value might grow—how its crediting rate will be determined. I'll explain some of the options in the following chapter. Once you know more about the language of FIAs, I'll go back and explain how the Walkers are using an FIA to meet their retirement income goals, in Chapter 7.

CHAPTER SIX

FIA GROWTH STRATEGIES

To understand how and why an FIA can grow, you should understand how they are meant to fit into a retiree's portfolio. FIAs are not meant to compete with stocks, bonds, and other investment assets such as commodities or real estate. Such assets can serve a purpose for most people, before and after retirement.

Instead, FIAs could be considered an alternative to traditional savings vehicles such as bank accounts, money market funds, Treasury bills, savings bonds, and traditional fixed annuities. FIAs have the potential to provide growth for your savings dollars.

As a financial advisor, I'm not allowed to use words such as "safe" or "guaranteed." Securities regulators get very concerned when those types of words are used, and I completely support and understand the reasoning behind that concern. However, I will say that FIAs are designed to provide the possibility of attractive growth without exposing you to market declines.

Are there drawbacks to FIAs? Certainly! As I state to my clients and prospective clients, there is no such thing as a perfect or risk-free financial product. One of the major drawbacks to an FIA is that you will not receive all of the stock market growth of the related index in most years. Also, you cannot access all of your money for a period of time without incurring surrender charges.

Now that I've gotten that out of the way, let's continue looking at some FIA issues. Your return—any return—from an FIA depends upon the financial viability of the insurance company offering the annuity. As an advisor, it's my job to help clients select insurers that will be around for many years, and are very likely to be able to keep all of their promises.

As I mentioned above, FIA returns are limited. Stocks might go up 30% or more in a good year—in bull markets, stocks can have several years of extraordinary returns. You won't get that in an FIA; instead, you'll get to avoid steep losses of principal during bear markets. This lack of full upside participation is the major cost for the "insurance" against losses in market declines.

Finally, FIAs can be challenging to understand. They're not like bank CDs or traditional fixed annuities, where you might be promised, say, 2% a year for the next five years. You will get a promised return from an FIA, but that return generally will result from a formula. These formulas vary, from FIA to FIA, but they all wind up producing a number in the neighborhood of zero, which might not sound like an attractive feature. However, some day you may find yourself in the midst of a severe and/or prolonged recessionary period in the economy, observing from the sideline as significant reductions in market valuations occur across the board and in every marketplace. At that point, a 0% (flat) return will sound incredibly attractive.

With few exceptions, you won't lose value due to negative market index performance, so the value of your FIA won't decline if financial markets go south. Keep in mind, with the purchase of any additional-cost riders, the contract's value will be reduced by the cost of the rider. This may result in a reduction of principal in any year in which the contract does not earn interest or earns interest in an amount less that the rider charge. You may also incur surrender charges which may apply to any early withdrawals. Nevertheless, the growth you can achieve in an FIA will be determined in part by the performance of financial markets. I'll explain how that works in a moment.

INFLUENCED BY INDEXES

As the name implies, the growth from a fixed *index* annuity are determined by index performance. An FIA might set its return from the behavior of one index, such as the S&P 500® Index of large-company U.S. stocks.

Alternatively, an FIA's growth could stem from a mix of several indexes, including foreign stocks or bonds or even other assets. You might have the ability to choose among more than one crediting method when you purchase an FIA. Besides using various indexes, FIAs differ in the way they translate index performance to the crediting rate, which is the buildup of your accumulation value inside the annuity contract.

WORDS FOR THE WISE

Here are some of the terms to know and understand:

Cap. This is the maximum you can earn in a given measurement period, often one month or one year. Say Bert Martin[36] has an FIA where the growth depends upon the S&P 500®, with a cap of 6% per 12 months. If the S&P 500® goes up 3% in those 12 months, Bert's FIA will be credited 3%. If that index goes up 6%, Bert will have a 6% credit. However, if the S&P 500® is up 10% or 20% or 30%, Bert's FIA credit will remain at 6%.

Now, earning 6% when the S&P 500® gains 30% may sound disappointing. You should keep in mind, though, that FIAs are not meant to compete with market indexes.

36 This character is fictional and his reference is for illustrative purposes only. Your actual experience will vary.

Instead, you should consider an FIA amongst all products available to you, and how they apply to your individual situation. By that standard, could earning 6% in the previous example sound good to you?

> **Participation rate.** The participation rate simply means, what percentage of the index growth do I share in? The above example assumes that Bert has a 100% participation rate, meaning he receives 100% credit for the first 6% of the growth of the index to which his annuity is linked.

I think this is a critical component in an FIA, so I make every effort to find a product that allows for a 100% participation rate. A participation rate of 100% isn't necessarily a given; that rate is often less, which can diminish performance significantly, as you can see below.

If Bert's FIA also has a 50% participation rate, his FIA will get 1.5% credited when the S&P 500® is up by 3%. He'd need a 12% S&P 500® return to get his maximum 6% credit for his FIA.

> **Spread.** As we saw above, in the example of the high water mark annuity, a spread is actually a reduction in the consumer's credited interest. An FIA that would provide 7% under the index-related formula would only provide 5% to a consumer, if there were a 2% spread.

This can be a worthwhile sacrifice, because in most cases an FIA strategy that offers a spread doesn't impose a cap. This means you give up the first part of the index growth with a spread but you also have uncapped upside potential.

For example, say your FIA imposes a 3% spread but has no cap. If the relevant index goes up 4%, you will earn only 1%, rather than all 4%. On the other hand, suppose your FIA is linked to an index that gains 15%. Then you would make 12%, even with a 3% spread! I've had many, many clients earn double-digit growth in years of strong stock market growth, and this strategy is one that has allowed them to do so.

Even with a spread in an FIA, your accumulation value won't drop. With a 1% index gain and a 3% spread, your accumulation value would be flat, rather than go down by 2%.

That said, some FIAs have both a participation rate and a spread, which I find to be unappealing. Generally, I want to use an FIA that has only one restriction on growth, not two or more. This is a major red flag for me in evaluating an FIA to recommend to a client; I'll explain more on this later.

Suppose that Bert's FIA has a 50% participation rate and a 2% spread. Then a 10% gain in the S&P 500® would provide him with 5%, under the participation rate, but only 3% after the spread. I don't like an FIA where a client is put in such a position.

Unfortunately, many insurance companies issue contracts that have multiple restrictions. I've reviewed such FIAs, owned by people coming to my office for a second opinion, and those are usually dissatisfied consumers. Remember, nothing is perfect, but some FIA product opportunities are certainly less perfect than others!

Typically, I prefer an FIA with a 100% participation rate, or nearly so. Consumers should receive a credit related to the first part of normal market growth, rather than hope for extraordinary gains in the financial markets.

CREDITING METHODS

Annual point-to-point. Caps and spreads and participation rates all serve to limit your FIA growth; that's the tradeoff for getting upside potential without the risk that your principal will reflect any market losses. All of these provisions are calculated for a certain period of time.

Annual point-to-point crediting measures index performance on anniversary dates or every 365 days. Thus, if you buy an FIA on November 1, any interest credited will reflect the index values on successive November 1 dates (anniversary) or on successive October 31 dates (365 days).

I like this strategy because it reduces mid-year volatility, which can have a negative effect on some other crediting methods. A 20% mid-year correction, for instance, would not impact an annual point to point strategy as long as the relevant index is higher on the subsequent one year date.

As explained above, your accumulation value will go up if the related index or indexes have performed well enough to result in an increase. Once that value has gone up, it won't go down if subsequent measuring points are lower.

> **Monthly sum.** With this method, the FIA has a great deal of upside potential, especially when you consider that FIAs offer no stock market risk. I've recommended this strategy since it was introduced in 2004, and for the most part it has served my clients incredibly well. There have been a couple of disappointments along the way—I'll explain how that can happen—but by and large this is a strategy that should be strongly considered.

The way this strategy works is simple in concept, but confusing in the details, so let's break it down. The relevant market index is measured monthly, not annually. Your accumulation value will not change for 12 months, as is the case for almost every FIA on the market. The difference from month-to-month is measured on a percentage basis, and then a cap (and, in some undesirable situations, a participation rate of less than 100%) is applied. For simplicity's sake, I'll assume a 100% participation rate.

Let's say your monthly cap is 2%. That's right, you can make up to 2% per month with this FIA crediting method. Thus, a monthly sum strategy offers the possibility of outstanding FIA growth. But keep in mind that no one crediting method credits the most interest in all market scenarios. Getting back to illustrating this method, say you have an FIA linked to the S&P 500®. Suppose, as an example, in Month One the S&P 500® increases by 3%. You would receive a credit of 2%—the monthly cap. Your accumulation value will not change because you'll need twelve months of results to make any changes. Let's say Month Two has 1.3% growth; you would receive a credit of 1.3%, because you get it all up to 2%, in this hypothetical example.

Say you get five more months of 2% growth or more. If the year ended at that point, your FIA would be up 13.3%: six months of 2% growth and one month of 1.3%. Yes, I've had clients earn 13% in a 12-month period. Recently, one client—a widow—earned 19% with a $400,000 account balance, so she received $76,000 in 12-month growth with no direct stock market risk. There have been a couple of years in which she earned 0%, too. During the crisis year of 2008, when so many people lost so much, she was happy with that 0% change in her FIA value.[37]

Getting back to our example, after seven months you are cruising along and "up" by 13.3%. Just when you're celebrating, some bad news spooks the market and the S&P 500® suffers a sudden 15% correction.

The tradeoff with this monthly sum strategy is that FIAs don't limit the monthly downside. One of your months shows a negative 15%. Now the credit is all gone and your monthly sum goes from +13.3% to -1.7%. Now you need a 1.7% monthly credit just "get even" and start showing growth. As I told you, nothing is perfect. Fortunately, months with negative performance anything like -15%

[37] The experience of this individual is not intended to be representative of what your experience might be and is no guarantee of future success.

are few and far between. As I mentioned, the monthly sum crediting strategy is one that has served my clients remarkably well over the decade-plus that I've used it.[38]

At the end of the twelve months, the positive months and negative months are added together. If it's a positive number, you are credited with that increase in your accumulation value. If the monthly sum is negative, you simply start the next year with the same amount of money. Your FIA value won't reflect the market loss.

In the financial panic of late 2008, a client of mine that we will call "Warren,"[39] had a -27% month with his FIA. Think about that—if Warren had directly invested in the S&P 500®, he would have opened his monthly brokerage account statement and learned that he had 27% less money invested than he had a month earlier. That could have spooked even the most seasoned stock market investor.

In Warren's case, he had slightly more than $510,000 in this particular FIA so a 27% loss would have cut his net worth by over $137,000 in one month! The good news is that Warren didn't lose 27%, or over $137,000, in one month. In fact, Warren had the same accumulation value amount that he had one month earlier.

Warren believes so much in what he did in 2004 (when he bought this FIA) that he's given me permission to use him as an example in this book. We will look at his history since the purchase date: May 27, 2004. He's become one of my greatest supporters; he has sent many friends and family members to my office.

In fact, Warren is so open about what has happened to him that he will even show his FIA statements to friends and family members because most of them simply don't believe what he tells them is possible. You might doubt Warren's experience as well, but it is absolutely true.

The bottom line is, if you are evaluating a monthly sum FIA with a monthly cap around 2% or more, I would give this

[38] The experience of these individuals is not intended to be representative of what your experience might be and is no guarantee of future success.

[39] A fictitious name has been used for privacy purposes. The experiences of this individual is not intended to be representative of what your experience might be and is no guarantee of future success.

strategy very strong consideration. Just don't be alarmed if one of those big negative months occur—remember that you were protected from that daunting market loss.

> **Monthly average.** With this technique, index readings are taken 12 times per year, once each month. Then the 12 monthly readings are added together and divided by 12 to get an average. This average is then compared with the index level at the start date to see if the FIA's accumulation value will be increased.

This is one of my least favorite ways of crediting an FIA. I've had clients receive no growth during years when the linked index actually gained. This also can happen with a monthly sum strategy but it's not quite as likely, in my opinion.

Suppose you purchased an FIA with growth based on the S&P 500®, but that index spends the first six months lower than where it started. Eventually the index recovers its loss and in the final month moves above the starting point by 5%.

In an FIA with annual point-to-point, you would realize a credit because the S&P 500® is 5% higher 12 months later. With a monthly averaging strategy, on the other hand, you would have a negative average for the 12 months and no growth for your FIA value.

To be fair, I've had the reverse occur. The S&P 500® started at a certain point, gained throughout the year but finished about where it started. All of those positive months created a positive average so even though there was no index growth for the year, the FIA showed a credit and my client was happy.

In that kind of a year (early growth followed by equal losses), you probably would receive little or no growth with annual point to point or monthly sum FIAs. I've found such years to be the exception and not the rule, so I stay away from monthly average FIAs. That's especially true if a monthly average FIA has a spread or a participation rate under 100%; then I definitely would choose another option.

Multiple years. Some FIAs re-check your accumulation value every two years, three years, or even five years. Here, you're gambling on success at one future date. Returns might be high, but they also can be disappointing if the target date falls when the index is down. In the event of a correction on the scale of 2000-2002 or 2008-2009, you could go multiple years with no growth. As a tradeoff, such FIAs might offer significantly more upside potential. That would be the only time when I would consider this option.

Fixed account. Most FIAs will give you the choice of switching to a fixed account during the contract period. In recent years, you've been able to get pre-set crediting rates in the 2%-3% range.

You might consider this choice if the related index has gained ground and you are wary of a pullback. However, you could miss out on excellent growth. FIA holders who took the fixed account in 2013, after a four-year stock market rally, missed out on high FIA growth when stocks shot up that year. Altogether, FIAs can be complex, so it pays to look closely before you commit your money. In some cases, you will find that an FIA offers an excellent tradeoff between low risks and potential growth.

During the almost 20 years in which I've recommended FIAs to clients, I've been very pleased by the way FIAs have delivered credits well above those of comparable savings vehicles, without the anxiety that assets with variable rates can produce.

Generally, you can choose a different FIA strategy every year. However, I've found it more favorable to choose one that has a higher potential for long-term growth and stick to it. Just as it's difficult to time the financial markets, it's not easy to pick winning FIA strategies, year-by-year.

CRITICAL COMPONENTS

At this point, I'd like to go over the two most critical components of FIA construction: Annual Lock-In and Annual Reset. I feel that it's vital for these features to be in an FIA you choose.

> **Annual Lock-In** means that once you've realized growth in an FIA and it has been credited to your annuity's value, that growth becomes a part of your protected value. This is an absolutely critical benefit and it happens automatically. Generally, the FIA owner doesn't need to make a financial decision to get the lock-in; it just happens.

The only way to lock in gains in most equity portfolios is to sell the investments and move to a cash position or buy another investment. Sometimes this selling will have tax implications, which can cost you a lot of money if you've realized a substantial gain. In a worst case, you'll owe ordinary income tax on short-term gains. Depending on your tax bracket, you could lose 30% or more of your gains to tax, simply trying to protect those profits. With Annual Lock-In, this loss to taxes won't happen.

Moreover, you could misjudge the financial markets and sell stocks at the wrong time. If your investments keep going up after you sell, not only have you incurred a tax and lost some of your profits, you will miss out on the gains you would have made by holding on. Annual Lock-In takes this off the table. Your gains are credited to your FIA value, they are now protected, and if the linked index continues to rise, you're still participating in the new growth. The tradeoff? In most cases you won't receive all the market gains. Remember, nothing is perfect.

> **Annual Reset** means that the value of the linked index resets each measuring period, either annual or monthly. To illustrate, suppose that an FIA's credits are based on the S&P 500®, which has a hypothetical value of 2000 on the annuity's first measuring date of February 1. If the S&P 500® one year later is 2200, you would realize whatever growth your FIA strategy credited. For Year Two, your FIA growth will be measured from an S&P 500® value of 2200.

Suppose that on the next February 1 the index is up to 2700—a good year! Assuming that your FIA was using a favorable crediting strategy and you received a nice credit, that growth for both years have been locked in. Now your growth for Year Three will be measured from 2700.

Now let's say that some global crisis shakes up the stock market, which plunges just as it did in the years 2000 and 2008. It really doesn't matter what causes the crash because, if you're exposed to it, you will suffer a loss. Lots of people will lose a lot of money, maybe money they can't afford to lose. In this downbeat example, let's say that the S&P 500® falls from 2700 all the way down to 1600 on the next February 1. If so, the S&P 500® would be a full 20% below where it was three years ago, and down 40.7% from where it was a year earlier. Amid such dreadful news, the good news would be that in every FIA of which I'm aware, your principal and all credited interest will be protected from this loss. You still will have your FIA value from the market peak.

Better still: the amazing thing about annual reset is that your growth for the next 12 months will be measured from the S&P 500® value of 1600. That's right, the S&P 500® is 20% below where we started three years before and you were shielded from the 40% loss the prior year. Going forward, you have the potential to make new money this year. The S&P 500® might gain 10% that year, from 1600 to 1760, and your FIA value would reflect that 10% gain, even though the index is still far below its initial 2000 value.

Suppose you're in a protracted bear market and a year later the S&P 500® is all the way down to 1200. Your FIA would reset and you'd get credit for subsequent growth above 1200.

Remember, nothing is perfect so you probably won't get all the growth from 1200, but your "imperfect" FIA has shielded you from the big losses of the prior two years (heavy sarcasm)!

Many advisors cannot get their minds around the value of this benefit. I have found that the FIA resets from the peak years of 2000 and 2007 to the bottoms of 2002 and 2009 have been of tremendous value to my clients, as growth from the lows have been excellent.

Now let's cover another issue with FIAs: moving parts. What in the world is a moving part? They are items that can be critical to the protection of your purchase and the issuing company's ability to keep its promises to you.

By moving parts, I'm referring to FIA provisions that permit the issuing company to make an adjustment once a year to keep the annuity within an acceptable range of growth. Generally, the issuing insurer will make very small changes on an annual basis; these moves typically are nothing like the price changes for milk (weekly) or for gas (daily).

What might such adjustments look like? Your annual cap on index participation may go from 5.0% to 4.9%—I've also seen a cap increase. In one memorable annual review, Warren received a double-digit credit and his cap actually *increased* the next year. To be fair he has seen decreases as well, but I assure you that overall, Warren is a very pleased and happy client.

In my opinion, you might want to avoid (I would never recommend) an FIA with multiple moving parts. I've reviewed FIAs with multiple moving parts for potential clients who bought them upon the recommendation of another advisor or insurance salesperson. I've never recommended any of these type of products.

An acceptable moving part to me is the issuer's ability to adjust the cap or adjust the spread if there is no cap. That is all, period. I will never accept allowing the issuer to adjust the FIA's participation rate—I require a rate set at or as close to 100% as possible.

Consider this. Suppose that insurance company A issues an FIA that allows it to adjust not only the cap, but also the spread and the participation rate. Believe it or not, I've seen this—I've even seen all three components revised in one year, and not to the client's benefit. There are many FIA choices out there, but you must choose carefully.

EXIT FEES

While discussing the fine points of FIAs, I want to discuss the elephant in the room: surrender charges. If Bob Brown[40] buys an FIA and wants to get his money back after a short time, he'll likely owe a fee called a surrender charge.

Such charges allow the issuing company to commit to a longer-term investment strategy because it won't have to plan for large early redemptions. Within the industry, some observers believe that these charges allow the issuers to offer better terms to FIA owners.

Many states limit the length of surrender charge periods to a maximum of ten years, so annuity owners

[40] This character is fictional and his reference is for illustrative purposes only. Your actual experience will vary.

can take all of their accumulation value and leave after ten years. If your FIA has a worthwhile income rider, you should never want to take your money and go elsewhere; hopefully you will stay with that FIA for your lifetime and realize the benefit of Income Allocation.

That said, it's definitely a good idea to have an exit strategy, if that should become necessary. In addition to limiting the length of the surrender charge period, most states have imposed maximum surrender charges. These fees are usually capped at 10% of the balance on Day One, with the percentage declining daily, monthly or yearly until the charge is gone.

As an advisor, I look carefully at surrender charges when considering an FIA. I know from Day One what's the most my client can lose, and that's only if we cancel the contract and walk away. A surrender charge is not a negative to me because it should never be an issue. Most annuities allow for a 10% annual withdrawal, free of penalty, so clients shouldn't need to incur a surrender charge unless there's a dire financial emergency.

By the same reason, it's critical that clients have adequate liquidity outside of the annuity if access to a large amount of money is needed in the event of an emergency. Brokers and advisors who don't like FIAs may make an issue of surrender charges, scaring many people away from them, only to keep their clients exposed to market risk. In some cases, those investors have lost far more than the 10% maximum annuity surrender charge. It might be my perspective, but I think the upside potential and the avoidance of downside risk with an FIA is worth tying up some capital for retirement income security.

CHAPTER SEVEN

RETIREMENT COMFORT FROM THAT CERTAIN FEELING

The retirement income goals of Adam and Beth Walker[41] were described in Chapter 5. Now let's revisit the Walkers and their primary financial challenge: gaining confidence that their savings will last over a lengthy, comfortable retirement. This the same challenge that millions of Americans are facing today.

To set the stage for this review, consider that your retirement will last for a very long time, perhaps as much as 30 years or more. Hopefully, you (and your spouse, if you're married) will enjoy good health allowing you to pursue your dreams during this post-paycheck time.

On the first day of retirement, most people start with a set amount of money that represents what they've been able to accumulate through savings and investments over a lifetime. At this point we must do something that most of us have little to no experience with. We will have to finance an unknown period of time (10 or 20 or 30 years or more), with a finite amount of capital. A certain amount of money has to be allocated over an uncertain amount of time.

For most people, during their working years—the accumulation phase of their life—they usually had a surplus of income over expenses. They were able to save some of their income to build a retirement fund.

---

[41] Fictitious names have been used here for privacy purposes. The experiences of these individuals is not intended to be representative of what your experience might be and is no guarantee of future success.

That dynamic changes dramatically as of the day you retire. Now, the average person's income doesn't cover their expenses and so they must begin living off their savings. This is something that many people have never had to do before, and now they must do it for the rest of their lives.

To say that for many, these first steps into this unknown territory are daunting would be an understatement!

FUTURE UNCERTAINTY

Adam and Beth face the same situation outlined above. The Walkers' source of fixed income is their Social Security benefit, which by their own calculation is going to fall short of meeting their estimated annual needs by almost $40,000!

When I met Adam and Beth, retirement was only six years away, and by that point they had managed to save $1 million. They were both still working and contributing to their respective 401(k) plans. With six years to go, they could have anywhere from $750,000 to $1.5 million for retirement, depending on what happens with the markets during these last remaining years in the workforce.

Even if the market cooperates and the Walkers retire with $1.5 million, an initial annual draw of roughly $40,000 for living expenses would mean that they are pulling almost 2.7% out of their portfolio in the first year, slightly below the recommended 2.8% as a conservative first-year withdrawal percentage.

Conversely, if the markets were to contract, and the Walkers' savings are reduced to $750,000, then their $40,000 annual withdrawal would mean that they were pulling out over 5.3% of their portfolio per year, almost twice the recommended percentage.

Thus, if the Walkers had followed the traditional Asset Allocation model—so much in stocks and so much in bonds—Adam and Beth would have had no idea how much they'd have in six years. Their financial fate would have been determined by the direction of the markets. Would it be safe to say that it is this kind of unknown that prevents many of us approaching retirement age from getting a good night's sleep?

BEYOND THE BASICS

Here's another thing to consider: whatever amount of money the Walkers have when they retire will be needed to generate income. That amount should be viewed as their income base. If Adam and Beth want to splurge on a big ticket item—a motor home, say, or a condo someplace warm or even a second home by a lake—that outlay will reduce their income base substantially. That reduction, in turn, could increase the chances that the Walkers have of exhausting their savings later in life.

When you consider these points, as I did for many years, trying to find a more certain way for my clients to navigate retirement, Income Allocation begins to make a lot of sense.

Why leave your lifestyle to chance during this part of your life? If you understand that your savings and investments are going to be used to generate income in retirement, why not use the smallest possible percentage of those assets to generate the income you'll need, rather than having to use the entire portfolio to generate the same income stream?

Adam and Beth realized the wisdom in this strategy and by following my Income Allocation plan, they were able to establish the income stream that they require, and in doing so they only had to employ 50% of their savings!

DEALING WITH DOUBLE TROUBLE

With Income Allocation, Adam and Beth addressed the two most serious financial risks to their retirement. As I mentioned previously, in my opinion Longevity Risk and Sequence of Returns Risk pose the greatest potential risks for premature exhaustion of retirement portfolios.

Longevity actually increases the likelihood of occurrence for all of the other risks. The longer I live, the chance that I encounter more market corrections increases, the chance that I experience the effects of higher inflation increases, the chance that I need costly health care increases, and so on. Year-over-year, longevity elevates the likelihood that I will encounter one or more of these perils.

For all intents and purposes, Adam and Beth mitigated both Sequence Risk and Longevity Risk with their decision to employ the ideals of Income Allocation! How? They chose to put part of their savings into a product that generates an annual income stream for the rest of their lifetimes.

With this decision, Adam and Beth purchased an anticipated monthly paycheck that will not decrease when one of them dies. A paycheck that is contractually guaranteed by the financial strength and claims-paying ability of the issuing insurance company, to come each and every month from the time they choose to start it. From that point on, as it relates to retirement income security, the Walkers no longer have to be concerned about opening a brokerage statement every month and wondering if the balance is going to be higher or lower than the month before.

Instead, they chose another option: they will be able to open their monthly bank account statement and see the same deposit they saw last month, and the month before, and will see next month, and the month after, etc. The Walkers have effectively neutralized Sequence Risk, because now they are not required to draw against their savings and investments for income every month.

Even if the Walkers experience a negative year with this vehicle, they will not be drawing from their investments while their balance is down. They can allow their investments to recover and not fret about the daily fluctuations of their portfolio.

PROFIT POTENTIAL

As mentioned, the Walkers used 50% of their savings to acquire this income-generating retirement vehicle. Going forward, Adam and Beth still have an investment account, which can hold up to 50% of their prior portfolio value. Alternatively, they can spend some of that remaining 50% on one of those big ticket items mentioned earlier.

Let's assume, however, that the Walkers don't splurge on a big ticket expense. Instead, they'll do what most people do: invest the remaining $500,000. Assuming no withdrawals, if Adam and Beth earn 6% per year on their investment portfolio, they will have $1 million in total savings in 12 years; if they earn an annualized 8%, they will restore their portfolio to a value of $1 million in 9 years.

Whatever their return, with any long-term investment success Adam and Beth will rebuild their starting balance at some point in the future. What's more, they still will be receiving those monthly deposits I mentioned above!

The bills are paid and from secure, predictable sources. Meanwhile, they have a sizable nest egg that they don't have to rely upon for living expenses in retirement—their portfolio is just "extra money."

In my opinion as an advisor, the financial strategy chosen by the Walkers is a much better way to go through retirement. It's not a lot different than what people experience in the years prior to retirement . While working, financial security really comes from earned income, while savings are there for emergencies or big purchases. Altogether, the monthly earned income that meets everyday needs is where peace of mind comes from.

Imagine the average family trying to operate with an annual income shortfall of $40,000 per year for a decade or more. Unless this family is very wealthy and very good at investing, the end result isn't going to be pretty. Yet many people begin retirement under those same circumstances!

THAT CERTAIN FEELING

Adam and Beth have chosen a plan that allows them to look at a contract and know, at any point in the future, what their lifelong income will be. Three years from now, five years from now, seven or even ten years from now, the Walkers will know the minimum amount of annual income they will receive. An investment portfolio will not provide this certainty, and in my opinion retirement security should not be left up to chance.

Think about being 60 years old, with the retirement you've dreamed about only seven years away. Wouldn't it be much more enjoyable to see that long-anticipated date approaching while knowing that you're going to start this journey with your monthly bills paid?

As you may remember, earlier in this book I described the 94-year-old gentleman who had been retired for 32 years with enough income to pay the bills during that time frame. He's never had the first thought of, "when will my savings finally be exhausted?"

Adam and Beth made the decision to avoid entering retirement with that concern, and they took action to assure themselves that their retirement was going to start when they wanted it to start, not dictated to them by a fickle marketplace. How many people who planned to retire in 2009 saw their plans changed by the bear market that ran from the October 2007 peak to the bottom in March 2009?

After a stock market correction that saw the broad market lose 57%, were those people still able to retire, or did they need to work another five to ten years? Adam and Beth removed that uncertainty from their planned retirement date, and I believe the majority of Baby Boomers should do the same.

FACING INFLATION

You may be wondering, what if the Walkers' income begins to lag inflation? If so, they can use part of their future savings to purchase more income!

Assume that 2030 finds the Walkers running short of money each month, due to inflation in the intervening years. Remember, they had $500,000 left over after acquiring their retirement income vehicle, and they still had six years to work and accumulate before retirement.

Say Adam and Beth have been very conservative with their investments, earning a modest return, so 15 years after our first meeting they are in their early to mid-70s with their $1 million portfolio restored. In that scenario, they could use part of that $1 million to purchase more income. At their older age in 2030, the Walkers will need to use less of their savings to generate future income because they will receive a much larger payout percentage.

ADDRESSING THE ANNUITY AVERSION

Having an adequate retirement income stream could instill confidence in your retirement strategy. Yet, I've heard many people say that they don't like certain financial vehicles, and annuities are among those vehicles.

Many advisors assert that they don't like annuities, but we have to question why an advisor would say such a thing. Re-read the above information in this chapter and think about why an advisor would not like a strategy that accomplishes what Income Allocation can accomplish for a client.

Chances are, such advisors don't like annuities because of the way they work in relation to those advisors' business models. As a fee-based planner, I'm not allowed to charge a management fee on assets held in annuities, and I might not welcome the idea that I may have to advise clients on this part of their portfolio for more than a decade without further compensation after the first day.

I'm held to a fiduciary standard, which means that I must always put my clients' interests first, regardless of how my own personal financial situation might be affected.

Yes, annuities pay a commission. However, that payment is based on the client's initial deposit, not the balance after five or ten years. Thus, an advisor isn't compensated for making money for annuity purchasers. I could be working on that part of a client's portfolio for a decade or more, while being paid only once. In my opinion, this is why many advisors do not like or promote the use of annuities. It's not that annuities are bad for clients, but rather that annuities don't fit the advisor's business model or that of their brokerage firm.

Adam and Beth have chosen what many of you reading this book should consider, the certainty of knowing what your income will be, at any point in the future. Based on the minimum contractual guarantees (in other words, the "worst case" scenario), the Walkers' annual income will be in the neighborhood of $36,000 per year minimum, beginning six years after their $500,000 purchase and continuing each and every year that either one of them is alive.

An investment portfolio would need to experience tremendous success in order to pay the same income from a fundamental standpoint. Previously in this chapter, I mentioned that Adam and Beth could withdraw 2.8% of their portfolio value in the first year of retirement. That is a financially sound withdrawal percentage that should allow retirees to make it through retirement without exhausting their resources.

Well, Adam and Beth would have needed to grow the $500,000 that they put into their annuity to more than $1,285,000 in six years, in order to generate the same $36,000 that the annuity will generate with its minimum contractual guarantees. That's right, if the Walkers had instead chosen a portfolio allocation strategy over income allocation, their portfolio would have needed to experience 157% growth in the six years prior to their planned retirement in order to generate the same income that the annuity's minimum guarantees provide for.

Considering this, you might ask yourself two questions. First, where do you feel that you have the better chance of securing the projected income stream that you'll need in six years? An annuity, with its minimum contractual guarantees, or do you employ portfolio allocation strategies that not only require 100% utilization, but that will also need to experience a level of appreciation that's just not reasonable to expect? Second, given these facts, why would any advisor proclaim that an annuity is a bad idea?

CHAPTER EIGHT

THE COST OF BUY AND HOLD

In the preceding chapters you've learned that Sequence Risk is a significant financial peril to retirees. I hope that you've come to understand that sequence risk is most perilous during the five years before retirement and the first five years after beginning retirement—making those 10 years crucial to retirees who seek to avoid a significant financial loss.

Similarly, I hope you've also learned that while longevity is a blessing, it can also be a risk multiplier. Therefore, creating a predictable and dependable lifetime income stream can significantly reduce the chances that you'll exhaust your resources prematurely.

HOLDING PATTERN

Your chances of retaining ample resources will increase if you invest well. With that in mind, let's examine an investment strategy touted by many brokers: buy and hold. This concept is simple—just hold onto your stocks and don't worry about the value of your investment accounts on a daily, weekly, monthly, quarterly or annual basis.

Investors should just "hang in there," because the stock market will trend up over 10 or 20 years. Historically, this has been true, but I believe that a buy-and-hold method can result in tremendous loss of current and future wealth.

How can you suffer a loss by holding onto assets that probably will move up, long-term? You can understand this paradox if you realize that one of the key ingredients of wealth creation is time. Compounding investment returns requires time; thus, disciplined saving and investing over long time periods can create great wealth. To illustrate the power of compound returns over time, consider Warren Buffett's purchase of many Coca-Cola shares in the late 1980s. It was such a large outlay that some people criticized Buffett, one of the greatest investors of our time.

I've heard Warren Buffett answer "never" to the question of, "When is the best time to sell a stock?" Indeed, that's been the case with those shares, which Buffett still owns.

By 2012, Buffett's annual dividend on his Coca-Cola stock was 50% of his initial investment back in the 1980s. Think about that: in addition to the increase in Coke's stock price, Buffett received dividends in 2012 that were around 50% of the investment he had made, roughly 25 years earlier.

PATIENCE IS A VIRTUE

That is a great example of how a buy-and-hold strategy can pay off over a long term. However, you should remember that Buffett wasn't using his portfolio to create income for current cash flow; he was allowing dividends to be reinvested, so sequence risk was not the issue that it can be for soon-to-be and recent retirees.

Moreover, during my time in financial services I have noticed that most people are not patient enough to own a stock for 25 years or more. Most clients want immediate results.

Instead, Buffett sat back and let time and compounding work to his advantage. Please remember this example when I talk about mutual funds, later in this chapter.

THREE FOR THE MONEY

By choosing to buy and hold Coke stock, Buffett engaged in *active management* of his investment dollars. That's one of the three types of investment approaches, along with the *passive* and the *tactical* (proactive) approach. Personally, I prefer a tactical strategy.

With the passive approach, you simply buy a fund that tracks a major stock market index and hold on. The premise: if most mutual funds don't beat their respective market benchmarks, it's better to just buy the index fund, avoid the extra fees and take what the market gives.

The challenge with this method relates to retirees and sequence risk. You'll basically get whatever the index returns, minus a very small fee. There's no management of your assets, so you'll ride the market down and take all of the losses, plus a haircut for the small fee, during a bear market. When the S&P 500® Index, for example, was down roughly 57% from October 2007 to March 2009, investors with S&P 500® index funds saw their shares' value drop by that much.

It's true that the S&P 500® has recovered all it lost and, as of this writing, has grown by nearly 200% from its bottom in 2009. However, how many people sold stocks at the wrong time and didn't benefit from this recovery?

In addition, remember our example of younger sister Jill[42] in Chapter 2. After an early-in-retirement bear market, the losses to her portfolio plus her withdrawals were so severe that the recovery didn't see her balance return to what it had been before the losses. For retirees, portfolio withdrawals are a game changer!

[42] This character is fictional and her reference is for illustrative purposes only. Your actual experience will vary.

FUNDS MAY HAVE FLAWS

If holding onto an index fund is passive investing, seeking stocks to beat the average is considered active money management. You might be a do-it-yourself investor, trying to emulate Warren Buffett by using your own investment skills to pick the Coca-Colas of the world. Or you might rely upon a professional money manager to pick stocks for you. Those professional managers often offer mutual funds, and many advisors suggest that clients hold several of these funds for diversification. I believe there are outstanding mutual funds for investors, with exceptional managers. Nevertheless, there are some mutual fund features that you as an investor should be aware of, because they could keep you from receiving the desired results.

For instance, look at a mutual fund portfolio's turnover ratio. This ratio shows the percentage of a fund's portfolio that is bought and sold on an annual basis.

In some cases, the turnover ratio can exceed 100%. For all practical purposes, such a ratio means that the mutual fund buys and sells every stock in its portfolio during a one-year time frame.

Now, the mutual fund industry is a huge proponent of the buy-and-hold theory. Doesn't it seem a bit contradictory that many mutual funds are trading stocks, rather than buying and holding?

Warren Buffett's success with his Coca-Cola stock, mentioned above, came from buying a high-quality, world-dominating company and holding it for over 20 years. Why would a mutual fund do something so different from what Buffett has done?

Mutual funds tell investors to buy and hold, yet many funds turn over a large percentage of their portfolio annually—it's a bit confusing, isn't it? Even a fund with a "low" turnover ratio of 20% would effectively turn over its entire portfolio every five years.

A CEILING ON CASH

Here's one reason why mutual funds encourage you to buy stocks and hold onto them: it's basically the only strategy that mutual funds can follow. The SEC requires a mutual fund to invest at least 80% of its assets in the type of investment suggested by its name. Thus, stock funds can hold no more than 20% of their assets in cash.

Consequently, stock funds cannot sell most or all of their holdings and move to a cash position in times of crisis. In my opinion, having the ability to go to a "risk off" position—waiting out a crisis by moving into cash—is critical to managing sequence risk, but stock funds must hold at least 80% of their assets in equities if the stock market melts down.

Ultimately, the mutual fund industry's advocacy of buy-and-hold investing is the only strategy that funds can follow, so funds encourage their clients to follow the same path.

FOCUSING ON FEES

Investors also should examine a conflict of interest related to the mutual fund industry and to the brokerage world selling those funds: internal fees known as 12b-1 fees. These charges provide more incentive to recommend a buy-and-hold strategy to investors.

Most brokers sell "load" funds: A, B, or C shares that pay a commission to the broker. Such shares typically call for an ongoing 12b-1 fee to be paid to the broker. (The name comes from the number of the relevant SEC rule.)

These fees, unknown to many investors, can range from 0.20% to 1% a year: $2 to $10 each year on every $1,000 in your fund account.

These 12b-1 fees can cause a conflict of interest because brokers are paid this annualized fee on a quarterly basis.... *and they get paid this fee as long as the client's money is invested in the fund.* Thus, if a broker's clients have, say, $50 million in Fund A and the broker is paid 0.25% annually in 12b-1 fees, that broker would be receiving $125,000 a year: 0.25% of $50 million. With a 12b-1 fee of 1%, that broker would receive $500,000 a year.

Now, let's say the economic news isn't good and we are in the midst of a crisis. If the broker encourages his or her clients to sell and move to a cash position to "wait this out on the sidelines," the broker would be sacrificing that quarterly 12b-1 check.

As you can see, in order to act in the clients' best interest and provide vital guidance that might protect their savings and perhaps avoid sequence risk, this broker has to go against self-interest and sacrifice income. That's unlikely and, in my opinion, one thing we need to fix in our industry.

From a practical standpoint, you can understand why brokerage firms and mutual fund companies advocate the buy-and-hold strategy. Under today's rules, a large part of their revenue depends on this approach.

On the other hand, as a fee-based planner, I'm paid quarterly whether my clients are in cash or invested in other assets. Most importantly, I'm paid to manage clients' money, not to keep them invested. The private wealth managers used by my firm can rotate to cash as a "risk off' position if they feel that conditions warrant such a move.

CALCULATING THE COST

Now let's look at what I call the cost of buying and holding. As I've mentioned, time is one of the key ingredients of building wealth.

Also, I've reported that the Dow Jones Industrial Average gained over 1,400% from 1982 to 2000. During such a time, when the stock market is on a nearly straight upward run of record proportions, buy-and-hold makes sense.

On the other hand, if you had pursued a buy-and-hold strategy from 2000 to 2012, you would have seen the S&P 500® basically go nowhere, giving you no investment gains. What's more, you would have endured two of the worst market corrections in history, from early 2000 to late 2002 and again from late 2007 until early 2009.

That 12-year period would have been a great deal different if you had earned a compound return of, say, 6% a year. As you've learned from the Rule of 72, that return would have doubled your money in 12 years.

Indeed, some tactical managers produced positive returns for their clients during that stretch of the 21st century by avoiding some or all of those two market corrections. They benefited from the upward market cycles without needing to recover from two prolonged downward moves.

This experience illustrates what I mean by "the cost of buy and hold," and why I stated that this approach can be responsible for a loss of wealth. Buy-and-hold investors lost because they missed a current compounding period.

UNHAPPY RETURNS

As explained in an earlier chapter, recovering from a market loss can be difficult. If you have a loss of 30%, for instance, you'll need a 43% gain just to get back to where you were. Lose 40% and you'll need to gain almost 67% to rebuild your lost value; after a loss of 50%, it takes 100% to break even. After the S&P 500® lost 57% from 2007 to 2009, investors needed to make a little over 132% to rebuild what they lost. Even more important than the lost principal was the loss of time. I'll explain this critical factor shortly.

For now, let's consider what many brokers were telling clients during those bear markets. Investors were told something along the lines of, "Just hang in there, it's only a paper loss, the market has recovered every time before, so don't panic and you'll get your money back."

There is some truth to this and I'm sure it goes without saying that we all hope it continues to be true. The market most likely will recover, but clients lose one of the most precious commodities that I am aware of, and one that cannot be regained for any price once lost: time. And time is one of the greatest creators of wealth because it is one of the essential components of compounding.

BY THE NUMBERS

The chart on the next page shows a 55-year-old with $500,000 to invest earns 7.2% annually, for this individual's remaining lifetime. Assuming no withdrawals, the principal will approximately double every 10 years.

Thus, at age 65 this person—whom we'll call Ava[43]—would have $1,000,000 in investments. This doubling occurs without adding another dollar of savings, but just by allowing wealth to accumulate—time and compound earnings are a powerful force!

From age 65 to 75, Ava will see that $1 million become $2 million, simply from the compounding effect, and from 75 to 85 that $2 million will become $4 million. In this

[43] This character is fictional and her reference is for illustrative purposes only. Your actual experience will vary.

example, $500,000 will become $4 million in 30 years if Ava earns an annualized 7.2% return and doesn't make a withdrawal. That's an eightfold increase in wealth through the power of time and compound earnings!

Now let's assume that another individual, whom we'll call Brett,[44] encounters a severe economic crisis at age 55, which results in a market meltdown such as the pair we saw in the 2000-2010 decade. Let's assume this crisis causes a 50% correction and our age-55 Brett experiences a portfolio plunge from $500,000 to $250,000.

In our scenario, Brett doesn't panic but stays invested, following a broker's soothing words. Once again, let's assume that over the next 30 years Brett has the same 7.2% annualized return as Ava earned. By age 65 (after 10 years), Brett's $250,000 will have recovered to $500,000, just like the advisor predicted. So Brett got his lost principal back and he was once again holding $500,000 of investments. Going forward, with the same assumptions as in our Ava example, Brett's wealth compounds from $500,000 at age 65 to $1 million at 75 and from $1 million to $2 million from 75 to 85. See, the buy-and-hold advisor might point out then—by staying in the market your wealth grew from $250,000 to $2 million!

The Cost of Buy and Hold

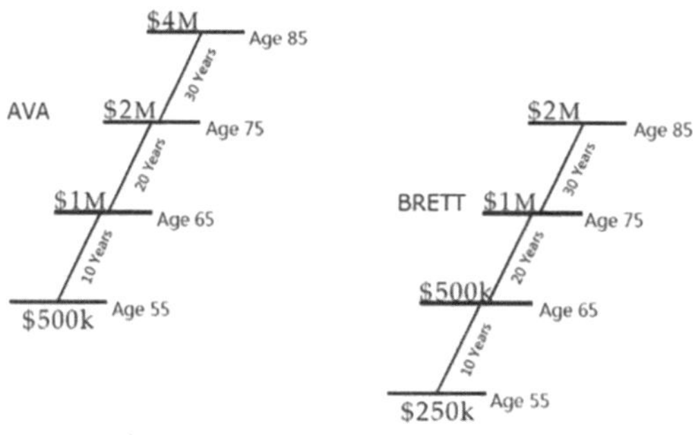

Assumptions: 7.2% Average Annual Return. No withdrawals From Portfolio.

This hypothetical example is shown for illustrative purposes only and is not guaranteed. It does not represent the performance of a specific product. The characters in this example are fictional only. Your actual experience will vary.

[44] This character is fictional and his reference is for illustrative purposes only. Your actual experience will vary.

There's only one problem with the above scenario, as you can see. Both investors started with $500,000 in these examples, yet Ava wound up with $4 million while Brett would up with $2 million—a difference of $2 million! Ava did so much better because she avoided the steep loss at the beginning of the time period.

This is the cost of buy and hold. It's not the amount you lose today, because if you stay invested history tells us, the chances are good that you'll rebuild what you lost. What you are not being told is that while you are rebuilding, you may be losing an entire period of positive compounding. In fact, the compounding period you stand to lose is the most valuable one, the final one that would benefit you the most because the growth rate starts from a higher base. This is the time when your wealth might grow to its maximum potential, for you to pass on to your family or to your favorite charity. Or, you might want the extra wealth so you can enjoy an extended retirement without concern about your finances.

As I pointed out in Chapter 2, with the example of younger sister Jill, retirement cash flow faces an even greater peril if you're taking portfolio withdrawals when a steep market loss occurs. You'd be exposed to sequence risk, which could result in exhausting your resources instead of rebuilding your balance.

Again, this summary explains why I have such a problem with the buy-and-hold theory of investing, with its set-it-and-forget-it mindset. I believe that tactical management, while not perfect, provides clients with a better strategy for dealing with economic and market crises.

By avoiding large losses, especially in that critical 10-year window (five years before retirement and five years after retirement begins), you can greatly increase your chances of a financially successful retirement.

BETTER THAN AVERAGE

As an advisor, I've found that some clients don't really understand the difference between *average returns* and *compound returns*. That's unfortunate, because the distinction is critical.

To explain why this terminology is so important, let's start with an example of two investors—Della and Ellery[45]—who both start with the same amount of money, and see which one actually has done better after three years. Della's investment results are -50%, +50% and +33% over the three-year period while Ellery earns 0%, +10% and +10% over those years.

Della's returns of -50% and +50% and +33% puts her total at +33% for the three-year period. That's an average return of 11% over three years. Ellery earned 0% and +10% +10%, which equals +20%. Divide the total by three and you'll get an average return of 6.67%, far below Della's average of 11% a year. However, this is an example of how misleading average returns can be.

As I'll show, Ellery actually winds up with 21% more money, despite a much lower average return! How is this possible? Let's look at the math.

Assume each investor has a $100,000 investment at the start of this example. Della experiences a 50% loss, dropping her balance to $50,000, followed by a 50% gain, which takes her investment up to $75,000.

Most people assume that a 50% gain after a 50% loss gain will get you back to break-even, but that's not the case. As mentioned, you need a 100% gain after a 50% loss to fully recover.

To continue, now Della has a $75,000 balance and realizes a gain of 33% ($25,000) in Year Three, which

[45] These characters are fictional and their reference is for illustrative purposes only. Your actual experience will vary.

will get her back to her starting point of $100,000. How is it possible to average 11% over a three-year period, and not have made any money? Because it's an average return, not a compound return.

Ellery, meanwhile, starts with $100,000 and earns 0% the first year, so he is still at $100,000. In Year Two, Ellery earns 10%, moving him to $110,000, and then another 10% gain in Year Three adds $11,000 to his total, ending the three years with $121,000. Ellery's average return of 6.67% soundly beat Della's average return of 11%, in wealth accumulation!

Therefore, when you are analyzing investment performance you should make sure that you are indeed looking at compounded annual returns instead of average annual returns. As you can see, the difference can be enormous.

WORST CASE SCENARIOS

While on the subject of analyzing performance, I'd like to address another very important process you should go through when making portfolio decisions: Stress Testing. This means looking at some critical component of your investment portfolio, primarily to see how it performed during a market crisis.

Other things to look at include the type of funds you own (load or no-load), how long the manager has been running a mutual fund, and the presence or absence of 12b-1 fees.

Let's look at the first point—examining performance in down markets. Ideally, you should own mutual funds that have been around for several years so you can see how the fund performed during 2000-2002 and also in late 2008-early 2009. You also should look at a price chart for each fund to see peak-to-trough loss, not just the annualized number.

For example, a chart of 2008 or 2009 will not show the full loss realized from October 2007 thru March of 2009.

However, an online interactive chart can assist you in this process; if you prefer not to examine such data yourself, your financial professional should know how to walk you through this exercise.

For example, suppose you own fund ABC, which lost significantly from 2000-2002 and then again in 2008. Is it unreasonable to expect the same thing from ABC the next time a crisis hits?

If you now have a better understanding of sequence risk, why would you want such a fund or many such funds in your portfolio? It may be time to make some changes!

Recently, I helped a retired couple who had the majority of their assets in funds from one of the major national brokerages. This couple's savings were mostly invested in the firm's "strategic portfolio." (By the way, that type of name usually is a red flag for me.)

The brokerage firm had sold the couple its own proprietary funds. Did their broker do this because they were the most suitable option for the clients, or were they better for the company?

Upon examining their portfolio, I found that none of the proprietary funds in this couple's portfolio had an investment history prior to 2009. To me, this was a major cause for concern because no one could have any idea how this portfolio would have performed during the last market crisis.

This couple was very uncomfortable being in such new, relatively "untested" funds, so they elected to transfer all of their investment assets away from this firm. Prior to our analysis, or stress test, the couple had no idea of this important fact.

TRACKING TENURE

As a final thought, mutual fund investors should note how long the fund manager has been running that fund.

If the manager is new to the fund and the fund has an amazing long-term track record of success, can that track record be trusted going forward? Perhaps not, as the person who managed the fund during its period of success may no longer be calling the shots. A good example of this phenomenon is Fidelity Magellan; star manager Peter Lynch left the fund after many years of success. The fund hasn't performed nearly as well after Lynch departed.

Fund investors also should find out whether or not your fund or funds have 12b-1 fees, which you are paying the broker or advisor. If you find these fees and you have previously been advised to stay invested and endure losses during a crisis, perhaps the presence of the 12b-1 fees will help explain why you've received that guidance. I realize that there is no certainty that tactical management will do better than a simple buy-and-hold portfolio. After all, tactical managers could make the wrong moves, selling and buying at the wrong time.

However, when you consider the importance of sequence risk to retirees and pre-retirees, I hope that you'll see the wisdom of establishing a foundation of predictable income. Once such a foundation is in place, you can try to navigate the tricky course of market-related investing with a proactive approach. If you use the passive or the active approach instead, you may find yourself enduring losses and then trying to rebuild lost wealth.

In sum, investors in or near retirement have many things to consider: buy-and-hold versus other investment strategies, turnover ratios, fees, conflicts of interest, manager experience, performance reporting, and stress testing. All of these issues can add to your sequence risk exposure.

It's my belief that understanding these concepts can increase your probability of a financially successful retirement—a retirement that you will enjoy for many years without exhausting your resources. Recognizing the risks and acting to control them can be vital for you and your loved ones.

CONCLUSION

THE IMPORTANCE OF INCOME ALLOCATION

In 2000, the tech stock bubble burst and the market crashed. In 2008, the housing bubble burst and the market crashed.

Since then, the majority of major U.S. indexes reached record levels, benefiting from what some have called a "financial stimulus bubble." Is another prolonged contraction in the cards? At the start of 2016, stocks tumbled more than 10% in three weeks. As of this writing, the market seems to have stabilized, but the future remains uncertain.

No one knows when the bears will growl again, but it's pretty much a forgone conclusion that the market will tumble sharply again someday as it looks to shed the "excess" from the system. If you are in the accumulation stage, that's probably not such a terrible threat, as stocks have recovered from every correction thus far. Indeed, steep market declines may help you build wealth if you have the risk tolerance to buy when the market goes "on sale" in the cyclical removal of excess from the preceding period of "irrational exuberance."

On the other hand, steep market declines can be terrifying for retirees. Then, you are drawing down your portfolio, without earned income to invest at low prices. After, say, a 25% market drop, you'll need a 33.3% recovery, just to get back to where you were. If you've taken a 5% portfolio withdrawal, for a total portfolio decrease of 30%, you'd need to gain more than 40% to break even. Sure, the market can and probably will regain that ground, but will any subsequent market rebound be too little and/or too late to have the effect needed?

In Chapter Two, I discussed the importance of accounting for sequence risk. If your portfolio is reduced by a severe bear market just before or just after you retire, you could be facing the majority of your retirement with a much smaller amount saved than you had anticipated. Research has shown that an early correction is far more detrimental to a retiree's financial prospects than a crash that occurs further down the line.

UNPLANNED FRUGALITY

Retirees who happen to retire at the wrong time—right before or right after a steep bear market—have two unpleasant options.

One, they may continue to spend as they intended, rapidly depleting their savings. The second option is to cut back spending sharply. In that case, their money may last, but such retirees may face a worrisome retirement, continually fretting about finances and therefore not enjoying all of the available time after they've stopped working.

COVERING YOUR COSTS

To help you avoid such unwelcome outcomes, I developed my Income Allocation strategy. Generally, this plan begins by allocating a portion of your savings to covering your expenses with assets not exposed to stock market risk. If you need $80,000 a year to pay your basic living costs, and you can count on, say, $35,000 a year in retirement income, you'd need another asset to pay you at least $45,000 a year. What's more, that $45,000 a year should be reliable for the rest of your life, no matter how long you might live. Once you have that certain $80,000 a year, to cover your living expenses, you can spend the remainder of your savings on pleasurable pursuits or invest those discretionary dollars for ongoing wealth building. Stocks might rise or fall, early in your retirement or late in life, and you will still know that you can pay your bills, today and tomorrow and the day after that.

LIFE ASSURANCE

Historically, the way to get steady lifetime income has been to buy an annuity. That's still true—there are many types of annuities available that can provide lifelong cash flow to retirees. However, in this era of low yields on savings accounts, traditional annuities also have scant payouts. You might need to use all of your savings in order to cover your basic living expenses with a regular income annuity.

Therefore, I recommend a relatively new vehicle for my Income Allocation strategy: a fixed index annuity (FIA). Let's break up the name, word-by-word.

> These annuities are fixed, rather than variable. As is true with a traditional fixed annuity, your principal typically is not at risk, even in a bear market for stocks.
>
> FIAs are linked to one or more market indexes. Thus, you have the opportunity to earn higher interest than you'd get with a traditional fixed annuity, if the underlying index does well.

Ultimately, FIAs are annuities, designed to pay you a stream of regular cash flow. You can choose—as many people do—an FIA that will deliver cash as long as you live, no matter how long that might be. If you're married, an FIA can make payments as long as either spouse is alive.

Make no mistake—even though many FIAs are linked to a stock market index, an FIA is not a direct stock market investment. When stocks have a good year, you probably won't make as much money as your cousin who is 100% invested in the market.

Instead, FIAs are designed to provide protection of principal with more growth potential when compared to other vehicles that credit interest to the account value. This is not a complete comparison of all features of those financial vehicles.

PROVEN PERFORMANCE

Above, I mentioned that FIAs are relatively new. That's true, but FIAs are not some app that was dreamed up yesterday. I have been recommending them to clients for nearly 20 years, with predominantly positive results. In fact, my client "Warren" could not be more pleased with his now decade-long experience of utilizing a fixed index annuity as a means for building wealth and generating a cash flow stream long into the future, even during periods of market turmoil.[46]

[46] A fictitious name has been used for privacy purposes. The experiences of this individual is not intended to be representative of what your experience might be and is no guarantee of future success.

COVERING THE BASICS

How does an FIA fit into my Income Allocation strategy? As mentioned, I want my clients to have enough reliable income to cover their basic expenses in retirement, regardless of what happens in the financial markets.

Thus, Income Allocation begins with a straightforward calculation: how much cash flow will I need in retirement, and how much can I depend upon now? If a couple expects to need $100,000 a year in retirement, for example, to pay their monthly bills, and they expect to receive $60,000 a year from Social Security, they need another $40,000 a year. (This assumes neither spouse will receive a pension or any other predictable stream of cash flow.)

In this example, the couple can buy an FIA that will pay them $40,000 a year, for the rest of their lives. The cost of such an FIA will vary, depending on their ages and current interest rates, but in my experience most recent retirees and near-retirees can acquire an appropriate FIA with a portion of their liquid net worth.

DISCOVERING TRULY GOLDEN YEARS

Once such an FIA is in place, backed by an insurer with a long history of financial strength, a retiree can be confident the bills will be paid. Even a severe bear market won't interrupt this cash flow.

Going forward, the savings not placed in an FIA can be considered "house money": dollars that are yours to use as you wish, without risk to your retirement lifestyle. You can spend that money on outlays you've had your eye on for some time, you can keep those dollars invested for future needs, or you can hold onto them for future bequests to loved ones.

Altogether, isn't that the best of all possible outcomes? A carefree retirement plus ample funds to use as you wish? While your peers may be anxiously watching the evening news, fearful of yet another stock market collapse, or living meagerly in a low-yield environment, you can look forward to enjoying your retirement for as long as it lasts.

About the Author

David Gaylor is a 25-year veteran of the financial services industry and has spent his career helping Boomers and retirees save and invest for their financial goals and retirement destinations. David founded Tradewinds Financial Group, Inc., in 2002 specifically to serve the wealth management and retirement planning needs of residents of the Miami [Ohio] Valley.

David takes pride in having protected his clients from the two worst market corrections since the Great Depression, and makes it his goal to ease the financial concerns his clients face on the journey to their retirement destination. He knows how important it is to find the right blend of growth and protection that is unique to each client, and therefore focuses on two main goals; making sure clients know the importance of protecting their principal purchase, and utilizing a unique three-step process to plan, protect and preserve retirement assets.

David came from humble beginnings and has a passion for serving the needs of the retired and those near retirement. Through family members, he witnessed firsthand the devastation that a loss of income can mean to the surviving spouse, and the difficulties associated with loss due to excessive risk, taxes and fees during retirement. He began his financial services career in the late 1980s, and in 1990 began to pursue his goal of helping retirees protect their life savings. David has been helping Ohio residents on their retirement journey ever since.

David is a member of the Million Dollar Round Table, the National Association of Insurance and Financial Advisors and the Ed Slott Master Elite IRA Advisor Group. Tradewinds Financial Group is accredited by the Better Business Bureau.

Going from the professional to the personal, David is a lifelong resident of Sidney, Ohio, and is married to his high school sweetheart, Mitzi. Together they have three children, Aubrey, Abigail and Brady, and one grandchild, Leia. His oldest daughter works for the family business and his son is planning to join the firm after studying finance and marketing at Wright State University.

DISCLOSURES

This publication contains the opinions and ideas of its author. It is intended to provide helpful and informative material on the subject matter covered. It is sold with the understanding that the author and publisher are not engaged in rendering professional services in the book. The information provided is not intended as tax, investment or legal advice, and should not be relied on as such. If the reader requires personal assistance or advice, you are encouraged to seek tax, investment or legal advice from an independent professional advisor.

The views expressed herein are exclusively those of the author and do not represent the views of any other person or any organization with which the author is, or may be associated.

Not affiliated with the U.S. government or any government agency.

This book has not been reviewed by, approved, endorsed, or authorized by the Social Security Administration.

The material in this book is intended for informational purposes only. It should not be considered an offer of any product. One might potentially use a variety of different investment and/or insurance products in planning for retirement. Everyone should consult with their own financial professional to assist them in determining which options are most suitable for them, based on their specific situation and objectives.

Any mention within the pages of this book regarding any particular product or strategy as a means of addressing retirement income concerns, is not meant to be construed as the definitive, only, or best available option for that purpose.

The S&P 500® is designed to be a leading indicator of U.S. equities and is meant to reflect risk/return characteristics of the large cap sector. It is not available for direct investment.

For any given financial concern, there can be multiple solutions that might utilize a number of different investment and/or insurance products. If the author demonstrates any bias toward a given product, strategy or security, it is because the author feels strongly about the merits of that vehicle in this application. As always, you are strongly encouraged to weigh all of your options and meet with a qualified, licensed individual in your area to assist you in determining your best option(s).

This book is designed to provide general information on the topics discussed. Pursuant to IRS Circular 230, it is not intended to give tax, investment, or legal advice of any kind. Please note that the author does not give legal or tax advice, nor should anything within the pages of this book be interpreted as such. If you have any questions regarding any of the topics discussed herein, it is imperative that you seek out a knowledgeable, qualified, appropriately licensed reputable agent, registered representative, investment advisor, or subject matter attorney, in the area in which you live.

Any transaction that involves a recommendation to liquidate a securities product, including those within an IRA, 401(k) or other retirement plan, for the purchase of an annuity or for other similar purposes, can be conducted only by individuals that are appropriately licensed and currently affiliated with a properly registered broker/dealer or registered investment advisor. If your financial professional does not hold the appropriate registration, please consult with your own broker/dealer representative or investment advisor representative for guidance on your securities holdings.

Please note that the use of terms similar to, or related to the word "guarantee," including all variations thereof when describing an insurance product, including Fixed Index Annuities, are based entirely on the fact that any contractual guarantees within the insurance product are backed solely by the financial strength and claims-paying ability of the insurance company that issues the contract or policy.

The contents of this book should not be taken as financial advice, or as an offer to buy or sell any securities, fund, or financial instruments. Any illustrations or examples presented are hypothetical and do not take into account your particular investment objectives, financial situation or needs and are not suitable for all persons. Any investments and/or investment strategies mentioned involve risk including the possible loss of principal. There is no assurance that any investment strategy will achieve its objectives. No portion of this content should be construed as an offer or solicitation for the purchase or sale of any security. The contents of this book should not be taken as an endorsement or recommendation of any particular company or individual, and no responsibility can be taken for inaccuracies, omissions, or errors.

Annuities are designed as a long-term retirement income product and are not designed for short-term financial strategies. Guarantee periods or annuity payments may be subject to restrictions, fees and surrender charges as described in the annuity contract. Guarantees are backed by the financial strength and claims-paying ability of the issuing insurance company. Fixed indexed annuities are not stock market investments and do not directly participate in any stock or equity investments. Market indexes do not include dividends paid on the underlying stocks, and therefore do not reflect the total return of the underlying stocks; neither an index nor any market indexed annuity is comparable to a direct investment in the equity markets. Clients who purchase indexed annuities are not directly investing in a stock market index.

The author and publisher specifically disclaim any responsibility for any liability, loss, or risk, personal or otherwise, which is incurred as a consequence, directly or indirectly, of the use and application of any of the contents of this book.

Trademarks: All terms mentioned in this book that are known to be or are suspected of being trademarks or service marks have been appropriately capitalized. The publisher cannot attest to the accuracy of this information. Use of a term in this book should not be regarded as affecting the validity of any trademark or service mark.

The author does not assume any responsibility for actions or non-actions taken by people who have read this book, and no one shall be entitled to a claim for detrimental reliance based upon any information provided or expressed herein. Your use of any information provided does not constitute any type of contractual relationship between yourself and the provider(s) of this information. The author hereby disclaims all responsibility and liability for all use of any information provided in this book. The materials here are not to be interpreted as establishing an attorney-client or any other relationship between the reader and the author or his firm.

Although great effort has been expended to ensure that only the most meaningful resources are referenced in these pages, the author does not endorse, guarantee, or warranty the accuracy reliability, or thoroughness of any referenced information, product, or service. Any opinions, advice, statements, services, offers, or other information or content expressed or made available by third parties are those of the author(s) or publisher(s) alone.

References to other sources of information does not constitute a referral, endorsement, or recommendation of any product or service. The existence of any particular reference is simply intended to imply potential interest to the reader.